AF254607

A MAN ADRIFT

A Man Adrift

An Immigrant Life from Spain to Australia

Alfonso Mora Almenara

Edited and rewritten by Manolete Mora

To Dad,
whose journey from Spain to Australia
made all our stories possible

Every man's life ends the same way. It is only the details of how he lived and how he died that distinguish one man from another.

— Ernest Hemingway

CONTENTS

Prelude to a Life

My father wrote his memoirs in English, his second language. He had no formal education, but he had something harder to teach: a storyteller's instinct, the irrepressible need to entertain, to embroider, to keep whoever was listening leaning in. His grammar was broken, his spelling erratic, his phrasing sometimes hard to follow. But his voice was never less than his. He believed, sincerely, in the old adage that you should never let the truth interfere with a good story, and his writings, whether memoir or fiction, reflect that. Fact and fancy, confession and invention, sit easily together in his pages. This memoir preserves that quality, because to iron it out would be to lose the man himself.

What these pages contain is not a historical record, though there is history in them. They are the story of a boy from a Madrid attic who wanted to be a bullfighter, fled a terrible civil war, fought with the Free French at sixteen, spent years at sea running contraband through postwar Europe, and eventually washed up in Woolloomooloo with nothing but a canvas bag and a lot of nerve. He was not a simple man, though he lived simply. He chased freedom sometimes at the expense of people who trusted him. He could be reckless, selfish, and occasionally dishonest. He could also be generous, funny, and surprisingly tender. The man who helped Jewish refugees reach Palestine was the same man who worked briefly for a London gangster. Most of us contain contradictions. My father's were larger than most, and he sang them at full volume.

I have reworked his manuscript by untangling the syntax, clarifying the sequence, trying to keep his voice intact while making it more readable. Where memory and fact don't quite align, I have let memory stand. That felt right for a man who understood that the stories we tell about our lives are as true, in their way, as the lives themselves.

He wrote not for posterity. He wrote because stories were what spiritually nourished him, and because he wanted his children to know where they came from. This is our attempt to honour that.

It begins in the Barrio de las Letras, the Literary Quarter of old Madrid, where Cervantes and Lope de Vega once lived and wrote. In those narrow lanes, the air carried the scent of bread and gunpowder, and boys learned early to keep their heads down and their eyes open. It was there that Alfonso's life took its first sharp turns and set out on the road that would carry him far beyond the barrio's rooftops.

Manolete Mora

PART I

Spain, England, and the Years of Drift

1

THE PROMISE MADE IN BLOOD

My story begins with the promise—one my mother kept to the Christ of the Great Power. This was the setting for a life shaped by faith and fate. Years ago, I heard this story. It seemed a stretch at the time. Yet it was true. My mother, Teresa Almenara Mora, was born to comfort in Córdoba, Spain. Her father was a celebrated photographer, well known in his time. Grandfather, Eleuterio de Almenara, was clever and liked to speak of the stars, reckoning men would one day walk on the moon. Still, I scarcely listened. He was distant kin to the Duke of Almenara. That didn't make me anything. He was decent to me. Stories were told of his darker side, though. It was a jealousy so intense he once shot at my grandmother. They called it love but I never did understand love of that sort.

In another incident, there was a horse and an argument with Sánchez Guerra, some bureaucrat. They fought a duel at dawn. Whenever my grandfather wanted something, nothing would stand in his way. His was one of a brood of twenty-four, though half died. He was wealthy. He lost it on cards. He lost it on drink. Once he wagered my grandmother in a bet. The Church preaches marriage as an unbreakable vow, for better or worse. She endured his ways until his end and shortly after, she followed. I do not know if she died because she was free or because she was broken. She was gentle—everyone said so. Ten years after her death, the family searched for missing papers. They said she took secrets to her grave. With permission, they dug her up, only to find her still whole. The neighbours whispered about sainthood and maybe the government made a note of it. The truth rests with her still.

My mother, a beautiful woman, had caught the eye of Julio Romero de Torres. He was a famous painter from Córdoba, and she modelled for him. They said she was engaged to Miguel Fleta, the celebrated tenor, though her heart was never really there. She complained about his features. His nose. His mouth. Little things that seemed important then. They weren't. Her indifference was really colder than her dislike. In the end, my father appeared. He was not born to wealth though of comfortable means. He worked as an accountant and owned one of Barcelona's famed cabaret venues, El Molino. His origins lay in Madrid. Why he left, no one ever said. Maybe he didn't know, maybe it didn't matter. Destiny or chance led him to Córdoba, where he met my mother. Her father did not approve, not even a little. The stir it caused was great. In the quiet of night, my father climbed her balcony, taking her away from her life before. Some said he stole her. Some said he set her free. My grandfather, armed, chased them across Spain to Barcelona. He never caught them.

In that city of lights and shadows, my father turned away from marriage. My sisters arrived anyway. He could charm almost anyone; however, he had two failings, a roving eye and a thirst for drink. No woman in Barcelona went uncharmed, no bar unattended. He lost his money on cards and lost our comfort on drink. He lost things until there was nothing left. Our grand house in Barcelona was the first to go. Then our expectations. Faith was supposed to last when riches did not. Yet faith can wear thin with hardship. That was the world I came into. I was an unlovely child, so much so that my mother spared all those that walked the streets my face. I cheated death twice. My large head almost too heavy to carry, my legs bent and weak. The priest at my bedside ready with rites, my cradle more like a coffin. I did not walk until I was five. The doctors thought of me as a riddle. Both babe and beast, they said. By luck or God's hand, I stayed alive. Father was learned, a university seal to his name. He was known once through all Barcelona, yet he fell from grace as a Don Juan falls. Mother did not fall. She stood steady. Steadfast, she believed marriage survived anything. No matter its trials, it was an eternal pledge.

Father had kept a mistress, which mother endured. Eventually, the burden grew too heavy and under the cloak of darkness she took us and fled to Madrid. Madrid received us—penniless, unknown. Meanwhile, the charity of strangers provided an attic room, more a den for rats than a family. Space was scarce so we slept in shifts. To Mother, it was still a home. The attic had its own kind of charm. We boasted running water whenever it rained, the drips forcing us to sleep under umbrellas. For air-conditioning, there were cracks in the walls. Our landlord never fixed them. Too miserly. The attic, cramped and dim, was a hard drop from Barcelona.

Mother worked at her stitching day and night. The noise of her needle work comforted us in the dark. She did not stop. Her hands did not tire. That work was our proof we could endure. Father, tail between legs, pleaded for return, swearing he would change. She took him back, not for his promise, since there was no other way. The Don Juan act ended. Not because he willed it, simply because there was nothing left for it. Yet the bottle stayed as his companion. He had been an accountant and a successful club owner. Now he became a gardener, from ledger to lawn. He fell and kept falling. All the while mother kept sewing. The needle was her sword. Two more sisters joined. We were seven in all: Pilar, Pepita, Rosario, Carmen and my mother and father. Seven in a room too small for dreams. There was no room for idle thoughts. Only for survival.

Our drama played out in a city nothing like today's Madrid. Our attic was humble. The neighbourhood was humble too. Yet our street had felt the footsteps of great writers—Miguel de Cervantes, Lope de Vega, Calderón de la Barca, José Zorrilla y Moral, and José de Echegaray. They all walked and wrote there, their candles burning late into the night. They birthed great literature under that old Madrid sky. History clung to that old Madrid quarter and greatness hung over our humble lives. You felt it between the stones. Some nights, you thought their spirits lingered, waiting for another sentence, another verse.

We lived on Echegaray Street. Tight and narrow, each paving stone set in memory of the writer of the same name. Directly across was the Teatro Español. The finest playwrights, the finest actors—always there, always working. Below us, the Madrid Sevilla bar thrived. Each night, it pulsed with song. Music rose up through the boards and drifted into the attic. Dancers stamped, singers cried out, rhythms and old notes and laughter mixed together. We took it in with every breath. The sound was a bonus. Sometimes it was all the entertainment we had.

Mother was deeply religious but burdened by having a son mocked in the streets. The doctors could do nothing for me. Then, a stranger spoke to her. There was a church nearby, they said—a relic inside, the Christ of the Great Power. Miracles were whispered. Desperate, she promised if the relic cured me, I would parade as the child Jesus for five years during Holy Week. At first, I could only crawl. I dragged myself across boards and stone and finally after two months, I stood. Then I walked. "A miracle," people said. Everyone who knew my story called it that. I had changed. From an unfortunate child to one who could win contests. My face transformed, my body straightened. My hair grew fair. I was not the same. Mother kept her vow, and I marched in the holy parade. One occasion as the crowd pressed close a bomb was thrown at King Alfonso XIII's carriage, near the Palacio Real de Madrid home to the kings of Spain since Charles III. Chaos broke loose. I should have died there but I did not. I stood in that crowd, once an outcast, now a child beloved— golden hair, standing straight.

Plaza Santa Ana was a short walk from our attic. On summer nights, it was a refuge. Well-kept and lined with bars, the plaza drew the artists and writers of Madrid. They gathered there, they talked, they drank, they watched the world drift by. One evening, the Mayor of Madrid stepped into the crowd. Pedro Rico Lopez, fat and proud, mingled with the patrons. I was a cheeky kid, so I asked him where he bought his beer. Laughter rolled through the plaza. From that day, whenever he visited, he waved me to his table. On those nights, I met all sorts, Madrid's characters. Writers, performers, men and women with stories. My forthright ways won favour. My open manner opened doors.

Old Madrid was grand and alive. Organ grinders played the organillo Madrileño in the streets. The air was thick with the noise of fiestas and the fever of bullfights. Spain was very religious. There were saints' days and endless festivals. Still for us, Sunday at the Plaza de Toros de Las Ventas was sacred. My father's pay was modest, and we scraped to look presentable for church. But Sunday bullfight tickets were not an option—they were a rule. Mother worked all week and still had to pawn the sewing machine head to buy seats for the fight. She would get it back on Monday.

For us, bullfighting was more than a sport, and it ran through our veins. We talked about it in the attic, argued about it, dreamed about it. When asked what I wanted in life, I said, a bullfighter. A matador.

One day, a wealthy man noticed me at Plaza Santa Ana. He said that when I grew older, he could guide my career in the ring. I believed him and it seemed that my plans would work out. Father, meanwhile, had long moved past chasing women, the cost too great. But he never put down the bottle. Mother took the burden—quietly, tirelessly. Yet strangely, I felt closer to Father. My sisters watched me like hawks, as Father ordered. Mischief was my game, and he saw the devil behind my smile. I slipped from their grip whenever I could. I was drawn to the streets, drawn to the wrong boys. They were bad news, but they were mine.

The gang of boys I ran with were trouble, my kind of trouble, ne'er do wells and alley cats. I felt comfortable with them, even when father said stay away. On my seventh birthday, I wore new trousers—long ones, made by Mother's hands. The first I'd ever had. I had five pesetas from my father. That was fortune enough. I was heading for my grandmothers for lunch, the first time I had gone out alone. Courage, I thought, wasn't just standing up in a ring. It was what you stood for. I would need it at my grandmother's table. Fate, however, had me cross paths with the gang. The boys said they were off to practise bullfighting at a ganadería, a breeding ranch on the outskirts of Madrid. One of those boys was a real troublemaker. He grew up famous, a matador, married to the ranch owner's daughter. I boasted about my birthday, my grandmother's lunch, and the five pesetas. That got their attention. They swarmed, tempting me. Skip lunch they said. Face a calf in the ring. I should've walked on, though their temptation fought hard against my father's trust. The temptation won. So, I went.

We hitched a ride on the back of a tram. The ride to the ranch took an hour. It felt endless. The makeshift bullring was a circle of dust. For twenty-five pesetas, you could dance with a calf. We had only my five, so we hassled the ganadero until he let us in. Four of us took up capes, ready to fight. The calf was wise to the game and charged at us, not the capes! They let it into the ring while I stood, cape in hand, unsure. I watched my friends play with the calf and would not be left behind. I spread the cape. I stepped into the dust. The calf was small, deadly nonetheless with twelve-inch horns. This was my first real dance with danger but the calf had seen many boys before. It lowered its head and charged. Not for the others—straight for me. It tossed me up like a leaf in a storm. Before I could shout, I was in the air. No sound. No parachute. The ground was hard and took me back. My clothes were torn to rags. The calf had done its work. I went to hospital, senseless came home late into the night. My father, agitated, had searched Madrid. He found me alive, battered. I'd escaped a beating from him by luck alone. After that night, he never trusted me in quite the same way again.

2

THE ATTIC ABOVE MADRID

Our attic above Calle de Echegaray is still sharp in my memory—bare, with leaks that we'd long since named "running water." By now, even the holes in the wall, our so-called air conditioning, had become old family jokes. What mattered more were the nights. At street level, Old Madrid was music and voices. The bars never truly closed, and the artists and patrons of the Teatro Español, famous beyond Spain, filled the narrow block with laughter and theatrics that wandered up to our rooftop for free. Night after night, guitar and song and dance slipped through the boards until dawn. Even when money was thin, the celebration and entertainment below never failed us. In this place, every draft, every echo, reminded us of where we were—at the heart of the city, just scraping by, but right in the current of life.

I started school at five but often ditched it to run with our gang of rough kids who had a knack for sniffing out trouble. That was their gift. Still, it was my fault. Nobody made me go. Good or bad, I picked my path. When you choose, you own the blame. You own the credit too. At seven, I was still skipping school for the streets. Outside the Teatro Español a man in a good suit stopped me. "Want to make some money?" he asked. "Doing what?" I spoke. A child actor was sick, he explained. They needed a replacement. "You'll have to ask my mother," I said. The man did. With the offer of good pay, my mother agreed.

For the first time, I stepped on stage and stood before an audience. I wasn't a bit afraid. I performed. Coupled with my looks, I impressed them enough to let me stay. As time passed, my roles got harder, and I eventually shared the stage with Margarita Xirgu. She was a famous actress and friend and supporter of García Lorca, who took a liking to me. We became friends; tea in her dressing room, her stories each afternoon. When the time came, she paid for me to study at the drama school.

Next to her dressing room stood the salon—a place bright with marble, mirrors, and the blue haze of smoke. Spain's literary elite gathered there to play chess at the small tables. Glasses clinked and every corner hummed with talk and laughter. One afternoon, I met Jacinto Benavente, Spain's most esteemed playwright and Nobel Laureate. He was sharp, neatly dressed, eyes quick under the lights. He waved me over and pointed at a man in white overalls, hunched over a chessboard. "This is a friend of mine, another writer," he said. It was Federico García Lorca. I did not recognise him nor understand his status. Not then. He moved his pawns with a dancer's touch. He watched the game like he watched the world—quiet, knowing, never hurried. Acting was not my dream. But the money was good. The theatre moved me from one theatre building to the next—Teatro Español, Teatro Fontalba. Days were feverish. Nights bright with footlights and the soft noise of a crowd. I thought about film. I thought about fame and riches. But success has a price. The masks change. The game grows dark. There is applause, and behind it, there is always a trick. Deception and manipulation live on the quiet side of the curtain.

After the trouble at the matador school, my independence finally came back—earned, not given. I used my earnings as leverage. "If you don't let me go out alone, I'll stop working," I said. They agreed. Money mattered. My freedom restored, I handed coins to the gang, and we paid our way back into the rancher's bullring. Twice a week, we trained, bulls new to the ring, sand hot beneath us. I felt it then—my calling belonged to the sun and the sand, not to the lights and stage. Still, loyalty to family kept me acting.

My name began to belong to the crowd and before Margarita Xirgu sailed for the Americas, she took my hand. Lorca was watching. "You are on your way to the stars," she said. "I hope to see your name in big letters when I return to Spain."

Time marched on.

In the heat of summer, we slept with doors flung wide. The cool air was a slight reprieve from the day's swelter, though some nights brought no peace. My father and mother argued politics—their voices rose and ran through open windows, out over the neighbour's balcony. She branded him a Red. He condemned her as a fascist. The quarrel spilled through the neighbourhood.

When father joined the working ranks, his side was certain, Republican. Mother never swayed from her monarchist views, an allegiance I could never understand. The adage ran like a warning—the wealthy fight with the Right. But what of those with nothing who do the same? Their quarrels filled our attic. Her stance cost her dearly when war came. Everyone knew where she stood. Secrets didn't last in close quarters. Words travelled, sometimes by the breeze, sometimes on scraps of paper. Unknown to them, a tenant scribbled their words into a notebook. Later those words became evidence.

3

WHEN WAR CAME

On July 17, 1936, I played with friends in the nearby Plaza Santa Ana until the early hours of the next day. The heat pressed in and back in our attic sleep never truly arrived. At five, before sunrise, explosions and gunfire woke the city. The sky itself seemed to crack open. We raced down the stairs and into the chaos in the street. Someone shouted, "War has started!" I was twelve years old, standing in the churn of the Spanish Civil War's first dawn. Neighbours and strangers scrambled. Ordinary men dropped their lives to join the lines for the Republic. Blankets slung over their backs, faces set. No one knew what tomorrow would bring. I watched each one, learning how the world changes.

The coup was planned, Franco's men sure of a quick collapse. The elite of the army had joined him. The Republic, though, did not fall as the people held their ground. Deep loyalty, hammered out by peaceful elections and hope, held firm against the monarchists and their old hunger for power.

The war had come and nothing in Madrid would ever be the same.

My father tried to join the Milicias Populares or Popular Front. They looked at his degree and sent him to a strategic role. "You're an intellectual," they said. No front lines for him. Instead, they put him in charge of the local Comité del Barrio de las Letras, the Literary Quarter, our neighbourhood. His job was critical—not rifles but words. He fought the Fifth Column, those who worked in whispers and shadows to break the Republic from inside. Sabotage, lies, betrayal. He took the job, but we stayed in the attic just the same. He turned down any offers of comfort or status. "I am a politician, a member of the Partido Socialista Obrero Español (Socialist Party), not a thief or a murderer," he said. "No personal gains. No revenge killings, not while I am leader. He meant it. Even as war turned, our life stayed humble.

Madrid's streets filled with people. They carried sticks, knives. Not many had guns. Against Franco's armies, they stood in crowds outside the Sitio del Cuartel de la Montaña. Just ten minutes from the city centre, that fortress became headquarters for a segment of the Spanish army. Under Franco, everything turned. He wanted the Popular Front gone, the Second Republic smashed. A quick coup is what they promised. What followed were three years of war. Blood. Hunger. Noise. Chaos.

Germany and Italy sent men and planes. Without them, the Republic might have survived. Madrid endured bombings. Explosions hammered rooftops all through the night and day. Still, life pulsed in our narrow street, Echegaray. Some cafes managed to stay open with singing and dancing. Crowds thick with song, music fighting against the bombs. People kept on with the old beat of defiance. The Republicans fought Franco's armies, but they fought something closer too. An enemy hiding in the city itself—the Fifth Column. These were shadows, never named, but everywhere. Mystery, fear, and betrayal wandering the streets at dusk. Madrid was a city on edge. The streets filled with people, many refugees from the countryside armed with sticks, knives, whatever they could find. Franco's force was strong, his rebellion launched from the fortress at Sitio del Cuartel de la Montaña, only ten minutes or so from the centre. Soldiers waited inside, confident in their power and command.

But even as the city trembled with fear and noise, life pressed in from quieter corners. War happened outside. Inside, in rooms untouched by shelling, another world waited. While bombs fell and crowds surged, the days held small secrets and silent beginnings. Nearby, a beautiful older girl befriended my sisters and, in time, invited us to her home. It was a large, quiet place shared only with her mother. The rooms echoed. There were vases and sunlight and old rugs underfoot. One afternoon I found her alone. Our talk drifted—slow, careful—until we unexpectedly reached her bedroom. The lock clicked. There was no plan, just the strange force that pulls the young forward. I joined her, despite my father's suspicions about my nature. At twelve, I did not belong there, yet I returned each day, drawn by what I barely understood.

The war grew longer; food grew scarce. People lived on lentils, sweet potatoes, gruel, and rarely, eggs. There was no meat. My arms thinned, my legs turned soft. Some days I had to rest, too weak even for the street. My mother noticed. She worried aloud, took me to the doctor—grey and blunt, suspicious of the toll taken by youth's passions. "He'll die if he doesn't eat," he said. Even young hearts can't live on love alone. He was right, but war and other hungers are not so easily counted. And so, it went on as did the war—hunger, longing, secrecy. Every afternoon, the house waited with its closed doors and a world too large for a single boy.

Still, private aches soon blurred into the day's larger fears. Whatever happened to one of us, the city found ways to remind everyone how close danger lay. When night came, hunger and longing made room for something heavier—survival. Madrid was unravelling. Bombs and shells tore through the sky day after day, night after night. The attic gave no shelter. Each sundown, we joined the exodus for the basement, what we called "the cave." Thick walls, musty air, the dim hope of safety. The cave was solid, the kind of place you trust when there is nothing else to trust. Everyone from the building gathered there—old men, boys in shorts, mothers hiding terror in their eyes. A family with five daughters huddled together, faces pale and watchful. The cave was fear, but it was habit too.

There, through the slow hours and the sirens, I sat with one of the daughters. The light was weak; her voice was quiet. Outside, the bombs fell. Inside, time stretched thin. Even as I kept visiting the older girl, I spent my days with her, wrapped in the odd warmth and tension of the cave, never sure when the shaking would stop or when the world above would return.

At the war's beginning, the Fifth Column slipped into government offices and flung open Madrid's jail doors. Criminals poured out, no longer just thieves and killers—now soldiers for a new order. They dragged suspects from their beds at dawn. They shot them against cold stone walls, claimed it was for the Republic, claimed it was for Spain. Father was president of our local committee. They came to him again and again. "Help us," they said. "Point them out." He refused. "I'm a politician, not a murderer."

The Dawn Brigade, on the Republican side, worked at night and at dawn. One evening while Father attended a meeting, their militia men came for my mother—hard men, no hesitation. Their faces were grim. They wanted a name, a confession, something to justify what was already decided. This was how war twisted ordinary days. Before, there were meals, and waiting for the news, and the small worries of poor families. Now there were knocks in the night, names on lists, silence after the doors closed.

In desperation, I searched every street for Father. Bars, alleyways, places he might slip away from trouble. I found him finally, sharing bad wine and stories with friends while the city shook. I spoke fast. News travelled quickest in crisis. Father pulled six men together. They ran with him toward the Brigade headquarters. No hesitation. Inside, the commander looked up—his own brother-in-law. The two men, once family, now divided by war and profit. My uncle was not there for the Republic, only for his own gain, cloaked in chaos.

Father demanded the truth. The uncle blanched, lips tight, caught in his own schemes. When pressed about my mother, he reached for a notebook. Pages full of charges. Domestic quarrels, overheard through thin walls, twisted into words like "treason." A list with her name at the top. In the end, my uncle yielded and secured my mother's freedom. She walked away, testimony unspoken, spared the fate of others whose names disappeared with the dawn—lined up at the cemetery walls, lost to the war and silence.

The Civil War, planned for weeks, dragged into years. Franco was furious. With his troops and foreign allies— German planes, Italian divisions—he circled Madrid. When the city would not break, the bombings grew constant. Day and night, shells fell. Families huddled together in the attic. There was never a night without danger. Madrid, though surrounded and half-starved, never offered surrender.

In those months, impossible as it may seem during war, I sometimes worked at the Teatro Ideal beside the parents of Placido Domingo, the famous tenor. But it was not like the old days, and bullfighting was finished for me—the ranch was lost beyond Franco's lines. Then news came: Federico Lorca was dead, assassinated. He had been a voice for the Republic, a face I remembered from the Teatro Español. Grief and anger came together. His death hardened my resolve. The Republic was desperate. Volunteers were called—sixteen was the youngest allowed. Most of my friends were boys with a taste for trouble, not sacrifice, but they stepped up. I could not stay behind, though I was only thirteen.

I had to find my own way in but the rules were clear, so I made my own. My father was not in his office, his desk was empty, the typewriter waiting. I took a risk some would call foolish. I typed my own authorization, forging my father's hand, the keys hammering out a passage from boy to soldier. There was nothing left but to stand among the men and hope I was tall enough to be believed.

"I, Rafael Mora, President of the Literary Quarter Committee, hereby authorize my son, Alfonso Mora, to join the brigade volunteers."
Signed, President of the Committee
Rafael Mora

I copied my father's signature, pressed the Committee's seal down hard on the paper. With the page tucked inside my jacket, I marched up to army headquarters. The stamp sealed my fate—they accepted me with a nod and a line on a ledger, no questions. I found myself again among my old gang. Not all made it. We were minus the one who'd later become a noted matador. With no ceremony, a truck waited outside, the same battered type they used for everything. They called our names. Eleven o'clock departure, no orders; only the promise of fighting. No parade. Only dirty boots, hunger in the gut, jokes edged with fear.

Back home, someone tipped off my father about my plan. Like a man possessed, he swept through Madrid, asking after me in bars and doorways, chasing whispers and half-truths. He found me an hour before the truck rolled out, grabbed me by the arm, yanked me from the seat. He saved my life. Days later, word came—the three boys I'd left were gone, killed on the line before they ever saw their names written up for heroism. Still, I needed to help the Republic. Madrid was choking. Franco's armies held the supply roads tight. The city was running dry—no flour, no meat, no easy work. The government was buried in prisoners, enemy soldiers boxed in with the rest of us. Someone in power dreamed up a railway, a line to bring food through. They took prisoners, set them to the rails, and put anyone willing to work under the foreman's eye. Luck carried me. I lined up for the job and got it—assistant to the foreman, young but eager, hands ready. No rifle this time. Just sweat, stone, and hope—a different sort of fighting.

My job was simple. I ran messages and carried lunch from a kitchen three kilometres off. The foreman was sly, a dark-eyed man from Andalusia. He used me for his own errands, sent me out on quiet roads to barter for bread or potatoes in nearby villages. Food for his own family, he said. It was always for him. But I outsmarted him. I made the rounds, scrapped with vendors, stretched my hands out for the last bit of flour, the smallest piece of ham. What I could carry, I brought home. My family ate first. The foreman got the leftovers, and I never apologized.

That was our life. Scraping by day after day, trading time for survival. Three years passed in that way. Each night Madrid thudded under Franco's guns. Each day the city shrank a little, hope pinched to the bone. Then the fighting ended. On March 28, 1939, Franco's troops rolled in, tanks rumbling over stone. That was a dark day, darker than hunger ever was. Their first order of business was to arrest my father. Politics and mercy never marched in step.

When Madrid fell, the boy I was fell with it. I was fifteen when I tracked down the wealthy man who years before promised to make me a matador, to back my ambitions for the ring. But war had changed the city and I found him gone—a bullet found him first. The world of theatres and fame had also closed its doors. Stages went dark, curtains drawn by censors and fear. So, I looked for work. The only place open was a restaurant, one of Madrid's best, run by the widow of a celebrated matador. She was kind, soft-voiced. Though her two sons and daughter were full of themselves, fooled by their self-importance. The eldest, fresh from Franco's army, expected Madrid to bow to him. He wore arrogance like a sash.

In the end, money ran thin for them, as for everyone. No charm or bravado could keep debt from the door. My job paid well, and the tips helped, but I worked with contempt. The matadors I served were legends to some, but only guests to me. I earned extra selling cigars and cigarettes under the table—black market deals, faces I trusted, hands that paid. Those connections helped keep me and my family afloat. Survival needed more than bold dreams and famous names. In those years, it took nerve, and luck, and knowing how to play against the airs of others.

Meanwhile, my father sat in prison, sentenced to twelve years and a day for his politics. That final day on the charge was a shadow—no one ever knew what it meant, only that it could be worse than all the years. My mother, who never claimed to know politics but understood people, went straight to Franco's officers. She spun her old loyalty like gold. "All my life I have been a monarchist," she told them, "and now you do this to me." They could not answer her charm. Perplexed, and perhaps swayed by my mother's persistence, Franco's men handed her 5000 pesetas—payment, they said, for her troubles, or maybe to send her away. She did not stop fighting for Father. I kept working at the restaurant, serving men I envied but could not respect, making good money in a job I hated.

A long time passed. The prison sentence seemed endless, each day counted but the last one—a day no one wanted to name. When mother's words finally landed, my father was released. He went back to work with less pride, more caution. I stayed at the restaurant, the taste of dreams and bitterness mixed in with every coin I earned. The irony was bitter: I stood near the matadors in the ring, not as a fighter, but as a boy doing what he had to, waiting for something better.

One day, an army captain came in with a Duchess. Sitting at the table, trying hard to look the part, he ordered cigarettes for her. But I saw the truth in the way his hand trembled over the bill. I didn't know him—his face was new—but his desperation felt familiar. He dined with nobility and had nothing in his pocket. I quietly said to him, "Sir, you are wanted on the phone," and led him away, slipping him some money from my black-market sales. It was risky. I needed the money for my family, not for an army man with borrowed company, but I trusted my gut. A week later, he walked back through the door and paid me double, his pride restored for a day.

Another day, Don Pedro Balaña, the bullring owner from Barcelona, came by. He was in need—cigars, good ones, hard to find. I told him I'd try. Later in the day, I returned with a full box, from my hidden stash. He asked the price, eyes sharp. I shook my head. "Nothing," I said. He didn't believe me. Not for free, he pressed. I told him I wanted something—something bold. "I want a fight in one of your bullrings." The table went quiet, then laughter. He stopped—looked me over, measuring. "If you've got the nerve to ask, you might have the nerve to fight. Come to Barcelona, and I'll give you your shot." It was the chance I'd waited for. All that mattered now was saving enough, scraping the money together, quitting the job, and crossing Spain. The dream was at arm's length, and for once, all I needed to do was step forward and take it.

Two months vanished. I spent what I earned, lost it to the nightclubs of Madrid—music, women, the promise of luck. Saving up proved impossible. Each dawn brought desperation. One night, at a corner table, I met a crew bound for France by way of Barcelona; broke as me, faces sharp, nerves wired. The ringleader was named Paco, a master at dodging fares, his wits honed by years of slipping past guards and inspectors. He had more nerve than sense—a risk, but I followed.

After the Civil War, Franco's men watched the roads. Police patrols stopped trains, checked every paper, peered into every bag. Travelers called it the new blockade—a wall of suspicion around Madrid. Still, plans began to stow away. Fresh clothes crammed into a canvas bag, I promised to meet Paco and the others at Madrid's Atocha Station, ten in the morning. I skipped work. At twenty to ten, I found them waiting, eyes restless, feet tapping.

Paco laid it out: "To pull this off, you need to be sharp. I know the tricks, you follow me. Don't be first. Don't be last." The rules made sense. He took the lead, I moved as second, the others behind us in single file—boys on a mission, half hopeful, half doomed. The hours crawled until eleven at night. The express train to Barcelona hissed and shuddered, rolling slowly out of the station. Paco ran. So did I, then the others. Doors stuck, but fists pried them open. We dove under seats, hearts bunched tight in our throats. The train trundled out, the city lights blurring past the windowpane. Madrid shrank behind me. I did not know I would not see it for the next thirty-five years. Only the journey ahead mattered, the rhythm of rail and the sharpened edge of freedom.

We lasted only a few hours before trouble came. The ticket collector moved along the aisle, eyes sharp and narrow. He caught us quick—no tickets, no excuses, nothing to offer. He sent us off at the next station. Guadalajara. Fifty kilometres gone from Madrid. The night air hit our necks and our pockets had nothing in them. Hunger gnawed hard and steady. We were lucky. The collector let us walk. He didn't call the Civil Guards. In Spain, everyone feared those men— violent, fast with the pistol, slower with questions. Worse than the Gestapo, the old men said. Careful women said it, too. Mercy was rare but that night, it came to us.

We waited until when a train whistle carried through the station, thin and distant. It slowed at Guadalajara, and our leader ran for it. We ran after him, boots slapping stone. I climbed beside him, high on the roof, wind cutting past my ears. A tunnel came fast and he grabbed my neck, jerking me down, hard, just ahead of the stone arch. I kept close after that. They started calling me the second. I didn't lead, and I didn't fall behind.

In Zaragoza, we reached the Ebro River, stained by the blood of soldiers from both sides of the Civil War. We washed off the train's dust and sweat and let the river take it. The day slipped by, two of us resting, two watching the station, hoping for a line to Barcelona. Word came back: a freight train would pass near three in the morning. It wasn't meant to stop. If we wanted on, we'd have to find a way. Our leader studied the tracks and pointed to a low bridge downstream. The train would have to slow there, just enough, maybe, for us to jump the flat wagons. He looked at us, his face hard in the last of the sun. "Be quick," he said. "Be certain. One slip and the train will take you under."

We didn't waste time on fear and the plan held us. That night we lay on the bridge, trading shifts, staring out for the train to Barcelona or whatever waited beyond. My turn came. I let my eyes close for a moment, maybe two, and the whistle hauled me awake. I shook the others. The engine loomed, iron and smoke below. Our leader jumped first. I jumped after, no thinking, no time for hesitating, hitting the wagon hard and holding on. I slept, worn out, and woke an hour from Barcelona, sky pale and unsure. We'd landed in different wagons; one by one, the train scattered us. Then a railway man saw me, and without a word threw me off as the train slowed at a bend. My comrades were gone and that was the last I saw of them.

An hour out from Barcelona, I counted my coins and scraped enough for the last fare. The beautiful city opened wide—bright sun, no plan, only enough in my pocket for a bus ride. Dirt clung to me from the rail yards, but I carried a soldier's bag packed with clean clothes. I knew the Civil Guard watched men who looked lost and hungry. Out of the station, I saw a boy and asked, "Where's the beach?" He looked me up and down, eyes sharp with questions. "Where have you come from?" he asked. The city and the sea waited past him.

"Madrid," I told him. "I came for work." I laid out my story—riding trains, skipping fares, ducking the eyes of the authorities. He liked it, the risk and trouble, maybe thought me brave or foolish. We walked toward the beach. Water lapping at sand, sharp wind, place to clean off the trip.

He asked, "Do you know anyone here?"

"No," I said.

He nodded, thinking hard for a moment. "I know the chief of the Falange—the Fascists here. He's a friend. He'll help you.

He took me to the Falange headquarters and named me to his friends. I told my story to the men gathered there. They clapped my back, called me brave. It was not courage—just not enough time to think, not enough time to worry about what might happen next. They listened as if I'd come from a war, not a train yard, wanting every detail, making me repeat it for each new face.

Soon, people visited just to hear my exploits, their intrigue touched by the shadow of police scrutiny in post-war Spain. The story grew with each telling. I ate a hot meal—the first in days, maybe weeks—and let the words tumble out. Their eyes stayed sharp, always watching for the police, for the patrols that haunted every street. But when night dropped, the crowd drifted home. The food was gone. I was left with my bag, no money, no bed, nothing but the dark city and the noise of my stomach.

The Falange headquarters, once a palace, now sat faded and still. As the rooms cleared, Narciso, the chief, called to me— "Come with me." I waited for trouble, but he said nothing more and led me out. We walked to his house, big and cold with old wealth. He had been imprisoned at the start of the war because of his politics. After introducing his mother, he turned and showed me the bathroom. I washed and he brought me to a room packed with clothes. "This will be your room for as long as you like," he said. "We're the same size, so feel free to wear anything." He paused, gaze steady. "But I ask for honesty above all. I'm not just the Falange chief in Barcelona. I'm also the Chief of the Civil Guard. Step out of line, and we'll have you in five minutes." So, I stayed in Narciso's house and wore his clothes. Word spread fast. Soon I was eating and sleeping under different roofs, everywhere a guest on the edge of trouble and hospitality.

Every Sunday, Narciso gave me bullfights and a little cash. Barcelona treated me well then. I moved among the city's best—the kind who talked high, smiled fine, and kept their politics tucked away. I met Mercedes, leader of the Sección Femenina. Young, sharp, father a famous doctor. She invited me home. I found myself in their house with the city's elite— bishops, doctors, men with careful hair and polished words. They drank, they talked, each eager for stories of Madrid. One guest raised his glass and said, "Without men like him, Spain might never have discovered the Americas."

And they laughed. I smiled back and let them have their adventure.

Mercedes belonged to another world. I was young and loved her hard. I had a little money and moved easy in Barcelona, but her presence left me restless, empty. It drove me—made me want to be something more, a matador, someone the rich could not ignore.

These people showed me that money doesn't always spoil men. It's hunger, the craving for more, that warps a soul. Those who never had must grasp and claw and won't let go once fortune comes. They'd sell their mothers to keep what they'd found. I watched and I promised myself—I would never be that man.

After two months, Mercedes weighed on me. I couldn't eat. I lost my laughter. Each day dragged. Change had to come before I lost her for good. So, I went to see Don Pedro Balaña, the man who owned the bullrings in Barcelona.

A servant let me in. "I've come to see Don Pedro." Soon, Don Pedro appeared

"What can I do for you?" he said.

"Do you remember me?" I asked. "You promised me a fight if I made it to Barcelona. Well, here I am."

Don Pedro looked me over, then smiled. "Ah, yes, the boy adventurer from Madrid! I said that in jest, but now that you're here, I'll honour my word." He pulled a card from his pocket and handed it over. "Take this to my secretary at the Plaza de las Arenas. He'll take down your details."

That was a Monday. I took the card to his secretary, Martinez, at the Plaza. Weeks drifted. By the third week, I'd nearly forgotten the promise, until I checked the bullfighting posters for Sunday. There it was my name in bold on the wall.

Plaza de Torres de Monumental
Saturday 22 June 1940 at 10:45 p. m.
Fiesta of San Juan and San Pedro
Four bulls from the Famous Breeder
Pedro Hernandez
For the Following Matadors
Joaquin de la Rosa
and
Jaime Gomez
Standby Matador
Alfonso Mora

Inside the Plaza, I asked the secretary if it was really my name posted. "Yes," he said, and handed me 500 pesos to rent a traje de luces, a 'suit of lights'. I picked a red and silver one. By the next day, Barcelona seemed to know I'd be fighting at the Monumental. I thought maybe Mercedes would kiss me at last. Now I had to prove I was a man worth her trouble, a matador famous enough for love.

It was my turn to win her. But I hadn't counted on the old saying—man proposes, God disposes.

I took a taxi through the city. Twenty minutes under the eyes of Barcelona, all stone and light. At the Plaza, I entered, paraded, saluted the officials, all under Franco's strict gaze. Monumental towered, wide and loud. I was sixteen, standing

31

behind the barrera, the wooden fence, while all of Barcelona watched—Mercedes and her parents too.

The first bull thundered out, horns sharp, body huge. As a novillero, new to the ring, I couldn't go unless a matador fell. I found myself wishing for it. The chance never came. But they called me in, finally. I swung my cape and worked through the gaoneras, each pass pulling roars of "olé" from the crowd. Standing between the boards and sand, cape in hand, I thought I belonged there.

Barcelona, it turned out, was not the heart of bullfighting. They loved La Fiesta Brava, but it sat strange there. I waited, biding time, hoping for a second fight. Weeks drifted into months. I knocked again on Don Pedro's door. He'd kept his word, but another start was a new battle. Hundreds like me waited by the ring. The real trouble—I had no Padrino, no Godfather. A Padrino is more than mentor; he is the key, his sword and name carried into the ring by the novice. Without a Godfather's blessing, a novice stays nameless, lost in the shadows where legends never rise. In the world of bulls, without a Godfather you might as well let the horns take you.

4

THE HORNS AND THE DUST

I grew tired of pretending. Time ran thin. One morning, I left Barcelona behind for the south, the true country of bulls. I wanted the dust, the old sun, and the promise I carried since boyhood. I believed the ring was where I belonged. Before leaving, I made my farewells. Mercedes was quiet, eyes wet. She said, "I love you," and clung to me. I said, "Someday I'll come back for you." Misfortune closed the road behind me. The money I had set me down in Sevilla. It was the heart of the matador's world, full of young men hungry for their place. My coins ran out quick. Soon I wandered almost penniless, chasing what little I remembered of the good times in Barcelona. I walked through the festivals and was bitterly reminded that every hopeful needed a patron. After the war, however, those pockets of gold had gone empty. Spain had come from tragedy to uncertainty, and every step on the road was paid with doubt.

With the last coins from Barcelona, I picked up a worn fighting cape. At night, it was my blanket. I learned to sleep under benches, steal bread, ride train roofs from town to town across Andalusia. By then, I was seasoned enough. But pain and harsh luck couldn't dent my resolve. I wandered far, to La Línea de la Concepción on the Gibraltar border, chasing a name that never showed. Tried every ring, more often tossed by bulls than taming them. Had I found a patron, I might have climbed further. Down here, every bull was raw, villages cheered for blood, and time ran short. In those moments, when the bull charged and the crowd roared, the thought of Mercedes burned in my mind. That memory kept my feet firm and gave my courage root.

I moved north to Salamanca in Castille where they tested calves to breed fighting bulls. There, I wasn't just looking for bulls; I needed someone to boost me to the top of the bullfighting world. Each exit from the arena left me more bruised and bloodied. From Salamanca, my journey stretched across northern Spain to La Coruña, near Galicia, only to realise I was squandering my time in Spain.

On a bench in La Coruña, I wept, alone and beat down. A young man sat beside me. I told him my story—how Spain had offered bullfights and little more. He listened, then said, "Why not try Mexico? There are fights all year." The idea sparked. But Spain was cut off, recognised only by Germany and Italy. Foreign ships were rare in Spanish waters and Mexico felt a world away

"How would I get to Mexico?" I asked.

"I'm headed there myself," he said.

"Really?" I pressed, hope stirring

He explained it plain. "Up north, between Ourense and Pontevedra, there's a place called San Gregorio. The Río Miño runs there—cross it and you're in Portugal. From there, we go down to Lisbon. Ships leave for every port in the world." Lisbon was far off, a long ride to the south. But what did I have left to lose?

I knew Spain was spent for me. I set my course for Mexico. Next day, I sold my cape, traded silk for train fare. We headed to San Gregorio, 300 kilometres gone, catching free rides on trains. I took the lead this time—old habits from hard travel. We rode atop the train to San Gregorio, where we searched for the river. At night, we found a spot—narrow, dark, cold. We stripped down, tied clothes tight, and went in. The current was strong. I was no swimmer. Still, I fought, arms numb, breath short, until I floundered onto Portuguese ground—alive, tired, shivering, but across.

Our clothes were soaked but there was no time to dry them—the Civil Guard was hunting us. We ran naked through the Portuguese territory, feet slipping on wet leaves, breath raw in the cold air. It felt endless. When we finally dropped behind a bush, the sky already grayed with dawn, we had a few minutes' peace. Hunger gnawed, but we were safe for a breath. Not long after, a Portuguese frontier guard woke us. His rifle gleamed at our faces. He barked for papers. I had none and told the truth. "We're escaping Spain, trying for Mexico. I'm a matador," I said, showing an old newspaper from Barcelona. The guard looked us over, eyes sharp. "You're a long way from Lisbon," he said. "This place crawls with secret police—spies everywhere, the war rolling through Europe." He didn't move the rifle. The world felt smaller just then, every road watched, every stranger a risk.

"I believe you," he conceded, "so I'll let you go. The safest route to Lisbon is through the mountains—slow and snake-filled, but the roads will have you caught and deported by police in no time." He then pulled a compass from his pocket and handed it to me. "Keep this with you, and with God's help, you might reach Lisbon. And if you do make it, I hope you'll remember me." He gripped my hand, not the other boy's, then turned and walked away.

We slipped through the night and slept in daylight, scraping what food we could from bushes and forest floor. After days, my companion saw the city lights and groaned. "We've been walking for days with nothing to eat. If we don't get fed soon, I'll die before Lisbon."

"We have no money," I said.

He didn't look back. "Leave it to me," he said, as the city drew closer.

We reached Caldas da Rainha. Outside a pavement café, we sat down and ate like kings for the first time in days. I worried over the bill all through the meal. When we finished, he leaned over and said, "Wait for me—I'm going to talk to the boss." He never came back. I waited, hungry for honesty, not just food. When I called the waiter, he said, "Your friend paid his bill and left long ago."

I faced the truth. "I have no money to pay," I said.

The waiter punched me on the nose and kicked my backside out the door. That was the last I saw of the boy, who'd been hiding his coins all along.

Alone, I walked south all night, just as the frontier guard told me. Compass in hand, no plan but to keep moving. My feet swelled and split, blisters opening. One night, spent past words, I collapsed in the brush and woke to poison in my leg, pain and fever clouding my eyes. I forced myself to stand, limped toward the first lights I could find, not ready to die among weeds and thorns. Night covered me as I staggered toward Carbahiño. Past the edge of town, a farm loomed, foreboding shadows curling on the walls. I knocked. An old man answered—wild eyes, headscarf, hammer in hand. I told him I was sick. He measured me with a stare, then waved me into the barn. "Sleep with the animals," he said. I was too feverish to care and fell down among cattle and sheep. Through the night his prayers wandered over me. Fever held me tight, then let go by morning. I woke with my strength returning. He brought bread, coffee, warmth. Before I left, he pressed a pencil into my hand. "Write this down," he said. "Antonio Ferreira Martino is a good man." I wrote it, a final tribute to a stranger whose kindness lit a night filled with shadows.

I left the farm and took to the bushes again, sleeping during the day, moving at night. Hunger drove me forward, feet aching, days blurry. The city lights pulled me to Oporto. By the docks, I searched for a ship to Mexico but found only fishermen and nets. The waterfront was no gateway west. The people were good. They shared their meals, opened their doors when they heard my story. Two weeks passed—kindness filled them, but I couldn't stay. I had to reach Mexico. Before I left, the fishermen pooled coins for my fare, enough for a rail ticket to Lisbon. But the Portuguese Secret Service drifting silently along the roads and police everywhere, I couldn't risk the direct route. Warned by the fishermen, I walked for the mountains again, compass pointed south.

They gave me a jar of coffee and sugar, plus matches and cigarettes. In the mountains, water was everywhere. I made coffee by my fires when I wished. Wild blackberries, sweet and thick, lined the trails. For weeks I followed this routine—coffee in the morning, berries by the handful, smoke at dusk. Lisbon felt just ahead, almost within reach.

I climbed down the slopes of an open mountain, night behind me and Lisbon ahead, lights shining in the black. Quickening my pace, I reached the city's edge at dawn. I stopped a man to ask the way to the port. He looked me over hard, suspicion plain. "That way," he said. "But don't go there in daylight. Secret police are everywhere. They pay for foreigners. Even your own kind might sell you for a few escudos." Thanking him, I spent the fishermen's money in a tavern to pass the day. Couldn't risk a boarding house with no documents. I waited in the park for night—the cover I needed—to try the port again.

At Lisbon port, I found three long rows of logs. I shifted some, carving a nook hidden from the guards, with a log door I could move shut each day. That was my home for three weeks. I slept by day and walked the docks by night. I didn't sleep alone. The wharf rats—big, bold—shared my shelter. Hunger made them bold and made me generous; I learned to share scraps, and they left me mostly in peace. Each night I crept out from behind the logs, searching the ships for a way to get out. Each day I slipped back to my fortress, waiting for a break, hoping to find the ship that would open the next chapter.

Three weeks in the logs and the dock rats behind me, a Panamanian ship called Dorothy slipped into port. Bound for Panama, I figured. From Panama, Mexico looked close enough—closer than it was. I decided to stow away. No crew I knew, no faces I could trust. The Dorothy docked on Friday. She would leave Monday at five a.m. I couldn't wait in my shelter—rats threatened more than the living. At one in the morning, I moved slow and steady, ducking port police thick as thieves. I saw no choice. I set my mind to climbing the mooring line. That was how I was to board Dorothy—in darkness, with the city asleep and the ship crawling with police.

I paced the wharf, scanning for patrols. Looking clear I climbed the ropes, hands burning. But halfway up, a sudden flash caught me—a policeman's torch, then three guns, voices barking for me to come down. With no documents, I had nothing to bargain with. They hauled me off to jail. Two months passed in the Lisbon lockup. My cellmate wore fine clothes and a sharper silence. He never gave a name, but I learned he spoke French and English. Spy, or something else, I never found out. They moved me under guard to Badajoz,

Spain—hundreds of kilometres away. There, in another cell, I met the same silent man. Released after another month, the guards told me to head back to Madrid or else. I had no home to return to. No prospects. Shaved and ragged, I drifted into Badajoz. A gypsy, a gitano, caught wind of my luck in the streets. He drew me into his camp. They gave me food, a bed by the fire, laughter and song in the evenings, a taste of belonging. But I was restless. That was not the road I was seeking.

The gypsies knew what it was to be lost and moving, quick with help for the outcast. I shared my story, my need to cross the sea. They found out about ships docked at Huelva, foreign flags, British-owned, with Rio Tinto mine guards and heavy fences. After farewells, I caught a freight train, setting out for Huelva. The country braced itself that week. Spain stood on the edge, war in Europe growing, the British presence at the Rio Tinto mines drawing every Spanish secret policeman to Huelva. Risk hung in the air. In Huelva, I found my way to Calle Gran Capitán. The street belonged to the outcasts—sailors, thieves, women with painted lips and men with quick hands. They would more likely help a stranger before the rich ever would. There I met a boy, my own age, who, through luck or fate, shared my name. I told him I was desperate to leave Spain for Mexico. We became friends on the edge of the war and the shift of the world.

Mariano Mora was his name. A Huelva boy, quick talk, all nerve, head of a little band hoping for America. With nothing left, I joined them. The country teetered on another war. At the Rio Tinto wharf, just two British ships stayed docked— our last hope. They were kept at the far end behind a swarm of police and fences, a place impossible to reach in daylight. The only way was through the water under the dock. That night, four of us agreed—we'd swim beneath the wharf, slip past the guards, and try our luck. The water was black and rising. The logs were slick. The tide climbed up as we clung and kicked, struggling not to drown. Forced to surface, we broke cover just as a ship pulled away. Only one ship was left, leaving the next day. We knew—this was it, our final chance.

When midnight came, we huddled together to plot. The wharf deck was hopeless—without a pass, it was suicide, and swimming under again would only get us drowned or caught. We were desperate and running out of luck. Then Mariano pointed to a rowing boat left stranded on the sand. "Let's take it," he said. "Borrow, steal, whatever. We can row straight to the ship." That was all he needed to say. We dragged the boat to the water, climbed in, and started the long row—heavy with minerals, heavy on our arms. In darkness, we drifted silent, easing up beside the ship's hull. We pushed the boat away, scrambled aboard, and hid beneath boxes. That night, sleep took us quick, and deep.

I woke tangled in dreams and saw red lights, thinking the police had come. I whispered to Mariano, "It'll be daylight soon and we haven't moved." He laughed quietly. "Don't be silly. We've been at sea for over an hour." Peering out, I saw nothing but water and sky. Tears came, sharp and bright—I was headed toward Mexico at last. The English ship steered us to Gibraltar. There, we owned up to the captain, who tossed us jobs and a berth. At sea, with work and a horizon to chase, I felt a deep satisfaction—more than relief, something solid. Every moment on deck, every wind and every blue swell, felt earned and good.

Among the crew, all English and strangers, I found comfort. The ship was bound for South America, with Gibraltar as the first stop—my hopes seemed set. But in Gibraltar, everything changed. New orders sent us for England with a convoy. I cornered a steward for a life jacket. He spoke Spanish, clumsy but kind. He said, "Don't worry, tonight there won't be a war." But by ten that night, German submarines swept into Spanish waters. Alarms cut the quiet. Fear hit hard—Mexico slipped out of reach, distant again, and I braced myself for another chase.

5

DANCING THROUGH THE BLITZ

The crossing to England felt endless, bombs falling every day. After a week, we reached Liverpool. The authorities sent Mariano and I and two other Spanish nationals by train to London, dropped us in an alien reception camp at Pembroke Lodge. Next morning, an immigration man called me in. He wanted my story, wanted to measure my worth.

"I want to go to Mexico. I'm going to be a bullfighter," I said.

He shook his head, laughing. "Son, you've come to the wrong country." He talked about school in England or sending me back.

"If it's school, send me back. Spain has schools," I said.

He pressed on. "Merchant navy, then?"

I shook my head. One sea crossing was enough.

"Pioneer Corps? Chop trees for the war?" he tried.

"I didn't come here to chop trees," I said.

He lost patience, shouted, "Well, what do you want?!"

I didn't answer. The road had forked so many times, I hardly knew anymore.

Two days passed before he returned. "If you stay in England until the war is over, Franco will fall. Then you can return to Spain or make your way to Mexico. Meanwhile, you can remain here or join the Free French Forces for the war." I asked, "What are the French doing here?" He showed me a book, explained they were training in England, getting ready for battle overseas—Syria, places I never knew.

Maybe it was adventure I wanted. Maybe just escape by any means. I signed up for the Free French Naval Forces, the Fusiliers Marins. Mariano signed on too. The other boys from Spain drifted away into the fog—never seen again. Mariano and I were sent to Barnes, London. It was just a ten-minute bus ride from Hammersmith. There, the French kept a small detachment, tucked away in the old part of the city, readying for whatever the war would bring next.

Before the war, this place had been lush—a club with swimming pools, courts, even a golf course. Now it was all gates and guards, a military camp holding men from every country. Two weeks in, curiosity pushed me to explore the grounds. I found a tunnel, damp and low, snaking its way to the Thames. Then came a wave of South American volunteers for the Free French. That's when I met Larrauro—a mulatto from Uruguay, sharp and warm. We became friends easy, and I showed him where the secret tunnel came out. Mariano got himself in fights with the English—couldn't help chasing trouble in the barracks. I kept my distance and stuck close to Larrauro. Here, every foreigner was sorted: army, navy, air. Every morning at nine, the sergeant lined us up, calling out jobs for the day, never saying what tomorrow would bring.

The French sergeant hated Spaniards. No reason given, but he sent Larrauro and me to peel potatoes in the kitchen.

I hadn't joined the Navy to peel potatoes. Instead, we slipped away to the tunnel, found a small boat by the Thames, and made it back just before lunch. The guards watched us round the clock, but we were allowed out three times a week. Three times wasn't enough for London. We went out every night through the tunnel, back the same way before dawn. London was vast and electric. In my French Navy uniform, I had more luck with girls than Rodolfo Valentino. There's a story about a Spanish writer who tipped every child he met in England. When asked why, he said, "One of those kids could be mine." I adopted his way of thinking. I couldn't speak English, but in England, the less you say, the more they seem to like you.

A month passed, then the blow—they moved all the South Americans, Larrauro with them. Mariano kept picking fights, and I couldn't stick with him anymore. I went through the tunnel alone. Two weeks later, they moved Mariano and me to Clapham Common, ending my London escapes. The new quarters sat between private houses, making it impossible to slip out without passes. My job was cleaning and kitchen work. Three weeks of this, and I'd had enough. I walked straight to the commander. "Excuse me, sir, but I didn't join the Free French Marines to become Cinderella." He laughed and sized me up. "Well, mon petit, I'll see what I can do." Two days later, Mariano and I were transferred to El Batallón de la Muerte—the Battalion of the Dead. A Spanish unit within the Free French Forces, filled with volunteers from across Central and South America, plus Mexico. Spanish Civil War refugees led us. Though they barked orders in French, the heart of it was purely Spanish.

Good luck came with the transfer—Larrauro was there too, and we became brothers. Half the South Americans in England lived on money sent from home. There was Enrique from Uruguay, devilish and handsome, impossible not to like.

He was trouble but the best kind of trouble. His well-off family in Montevideo sent him two hundred pounds monthly—a fortune.

I asked him once, "Your family's rich. Why join this war?"

He grinned. "The police back home don't like my politics. I had to leave."

Simple as that. Politics or bullets—sometimes the choice comes down to the same thing.

Our French uniforms were navy blue with white and blue striped undershirts and white collars trimmed with three stripes. We washed our uniforms daily, but I never saw Enrique's hands touch water. He stayed immaculate without effort.

"How come I've never seen you wash your clothes yet you're always clean?" I asked him one day.

He flashed his sly grin. "Why should I wash my clothes when someone else can?"

Later I learned his trick—he'd swap his dirty uniform for clean ones hanging on the line. Enrique was full of such schemes, always with a story, always keeping things alive around the barracks.

We had our own magazine, all in Spanish, packed with stories from the battalion. One made the front page—about me, the youngest at sixteen, still green about the world but quick to learn. I loved to dance. Whenever I could get away, I was at the dancehalls, mastering the tango and the paso doble. The paso doble carried the spirit of the bullfight—all drama and grace and the nearness of death. On the dance floor, I channeled what I'd dreamed of in the ring.

Our base was in Camberley. They held dances twice a week. In Reading, a bigger town nearby, there were dances every night. The music and the girls made the war feel distant, like something happening to other people in other places. In the early forties, as the English belatedly discovered

Christianity, they naturally embraced the Spanish and South American rhythms that came with it, bringing the tango to every dance hall in England. War had awakened something deeper than faith—it had awakened their hips.

So, the magazine story went. I was in Reading that night, where the dance halls never emptied. I spotted a stunning girl sitting alone and asked her to dance. Mary was phenomenal—we danced until dawn. She was a professional, from the cabaret theatres, otherworldly beautiful. We became fast friends. She gave me a large photo of herself. Soon every soldier was begging me for an introduction. But there are two things you never do: introduce your girl to another man or lend your horse.

Mary and I grew closer. She kept her respectability, though she let me kiss her once, rare in England it seemed. After a month of handholding, we went to the cinema, then for drinks. Past closing time, spirits high, we found ourselves alone in a dimly lit park. The blackouts made it perfect cover. She finally allowed a kiss. As passion took over and I ventured further, I discovered Mary had more to offer than I'd bargained for. I ran back to Camberley—my first strategic retreat of the war. My story became the barracks joke for weeks—not just on me, because they'd all been fooled too.

Camberley was a quaint village, but large enough to train Brits, Canadians, Scots, and Free French troops, alongside the Auxiliary Territorial Service—the women's branch of the British Army. These women were from another world, both friendly and fetching. I spent more time with the ATS than with my own unit. Geography made it convenient.

Our camp had a jail that would have impressed the Spanish Inquisition. It was the coldest place I'd ever seen— prisoners tied like mad dogs day and night, their souls frozen worse than their bodies. I doubted the British knew what they had on their soil, or they wouldn't have stood for it. Guard duty fell to us, Free French marines, army, air force. Twice a week, four solitary hours with a rifle, orders to shoot first and question climbers later. Entry required passwords whispered through the dark. One midnight shift, the yard filled with cold, damp fog so thick I lost sight of my own hands. Standing guard there was like watching over a ghostly abyss.

Within those walls, prisoners roamed free. Guard duty reminded me of those old Spanish horror films where someone might slip a knife between your ribs without warning. I was young and hardly ready to die in such a place. Armed with a rifle, I couldn't watch behind me, so every step forward meant a glance backward, watching for attack.

It was a bitter cold night at two in the morning when a loud bang startled me at the gate. I rushed over, rifle ready, and heard a drunken voice shouting, "I'm the commander of this camp and I want to get in."

I called back, "Password first."

He banged again, refusing. I cocked the rifle and fired into the air. The next bullet was ready for the commander himself. The prison security guard, hearing the shot, came quickly. He opened the gate and left me at my post.

A week later, the French officers summoned me.

"Why did you fire at the commander?" one asked.

"I was ordered not to let anyone pass without the password," I replied.

"Had it been General de Gaulle, I'd have done the same."

They murmured among themselves and soon closed the case. A week later, I received a promotion and a stripe. Not bad for a seventeen-year-old. The commander was never seen in the camp again.

Each week I had leave and would head to London. My single stripe swelled my chest like I was a general. England, even in wartime, struck me as democratic and this was a stark contrast to Spain where ranks stuck to their own kind. I went to the Seven Seas Club, a place for high-ranking officers that never questioned my presence. This freedom was unknown in Spain. All my life I'd been poor, but I found myself drawn to the wealthy. Maybe that's why I'd dreamed of becoming a bullfighter. My French and English were rough but at the club I met a lieutenant from the British Air Force. A society girl, daughter of a lord. I was just a corporal, a nobody ready to fall for her. She enjoyed my company, but her wealth made me uneasy. She had to cover all our expenses. My pay from the Free French Forces was seven pounds every fortnight. Not enough for a lord's daughter.

In the vibrant yet seedy streets of Soho I found a bar. The French House. I went in Friday for a beer, and an old lady came up to me. She spoke French and asked my age. She saw how young I was. She saw my stripe and insisted on buying my drinks. When I left, she gave me twenty pounds. This was good. I had plans with the lovely lieutenant that weekend.

We stayed at the Savoy Hotel, and we were happy there together. We lost ourselves in the weekend. Sunday evening, I had to go back to Camberley and that week I got a letter from the old lady. Friday my captain called me. He said I had a visitor outside. The old lady was there in her car with a chauffeur. She took me to her mansion in London and there was a party though it was all old women. The youngest looked centuries old but I was polite with the old lady, my patron now. She had titles and painted famous people. She did Roosevelt once for forty thousand pounds. She kept my wallet thick with notes. Parcels and money came to the camp all week and her affection grew, becoming a burden. I saw her as a grandmother. She clung to me out of jealousy. I told her about the beautiful lieutenant in the British Air Force. It made no difference. The old aristocrat stayed fixed in her feelings.

Back at camp one cold, foggy morning, we were drawn into manoeuvres. The Free French were to defend Camberley from the British troops playing Germans. They stationed us in a trench by the road, waiting for the German attack, armed with blank bullets that could sting at close range. We hunkered down and the miserable weather dragged. The South Americans started ribbing each other and my friend Larrauro turned his jokes on me. I didn't find it funny. "Europeans have no guts," he said. I ignored him. He poked at the Spaniards and the Civil War. I had stayed silent until he claimed no one in Spain had guts. That snapped my patience. "Before your people set foot in America, the Indians were there, braver than you. And who conquered them? The Spanish. So shut up!"

His taunts continued and my anger boiled over. "I'll show you we Spaniards have guts," I said and loaded my rifle and fired at his groin in a heated moment. The gunshot drew a crowd. He told the commander it was an accident. For that, I got three months in the very prison I'd guarded. Soon after, the camp magazine featured me on the front page with the headline: "The Kid Shot His Best Friend." From then on, they called me The Kid.

Mariano, who fled Spain with me, told the old lady about my imprisonment. She was upset so with her connections and she secured my release after two weeks. I was grateful though sometimes I wished I'd served my sentence. It would have freed me from her clutches. My life became miserable. She even wanted marriage. I once made a remark to her I later regretted—especially after she died soon after. I might have been a millionaire. But youth and foolishness were my companions then. Every Friday, her car fetched me from camp to London. Life with her was a constant surveillance. Every move watched. She dragged me to fancy restaurants and clubs, insisting we dance before all. It was absurd—she fancied herself Ginger Rogers. One evening, not long before her final departure, as we danced at a noted London spot, someone tapped my shoulder, asking to cut in. I turned and there she was, my beautiful girlfriend, the lieutenant. I dropped my dance partner to join her. The world seemed to stop. The old lady, enraged, slapped my girlfriend. That was the breaking point. My girlfriend stormed out and a week later, she was posted overseas. I later learned she died in action. Three weeks after, the old lady passed away, heartbroken.

As we mourned, others too sought escape from their losses. During the war, many Spanish political refugees found solace in England. They had an expatriate community centre in Notting Hill Gate. They called it Hogar Español. I visited one day, along with compatriots. Everyone was surprised by my French uniform. They invited us to meet Dr. Juan Negrín López. He was the Prime Minister of the Spanish Republican Government in exile. We would dine at the Spanish Ambassador's residence.

Two weeks later, my time in England was to end. I was to be sent abroad. Training wrapped up quickly. One night they rallied us. They were vague about our mission. Only when we reached the London dock did we realize it. We boarded a naval ship. It wasn't just another drill. We were heading into real combat in Syria with the Free French Brigade of the Orient. Mariano seemed fearless in England. But at the battlefront he stayed close. In the thick of fighting, anyone claiming they weren't terrified was lying. On the battlefront you either live or you don't. Kill or be killed.

My time at war isn't worth mentioning much. I wasn't brave. I wasn't a coward either. I followed orders and those duties weren't always easy. We spent what felt like eternity in hellish deployments. The Battle for Keren under the command of General Monclar, since we were marines. The air was thick with tension. Sometimes we fought fellow Frenchmen who sided with Vichy France. Then the dreaded happened. Half our battalion was lost in one assault. Many died in battle. Others took their own lives, knowing that as neutrals, capture meant execution. We didn't take prisoners either. Shrapnel wounded me in the chin and head. Our Spanish-speaking battalion was decimated. Those of us left were sent back to England. To Camberley. Defeated and weary.

One week, I escaped to a London dancehall, the Hammersmith Palais de Danse. I was dancing with a pretty girl when a redhead interrupted us. You don't refuse a cut-in, so we swayed for a bit until another woman tapped me. She was large. She was the redhead's sister. They took turns with me, leaving no chance to dance with anyone else. If you have no bread, biscuits will do, as the Spanish say. After the dance, I escorted the redhead home. Her name was Dorothy. She introduced me to her family, including a man I mistook for her grandfather. He was her boyfriend. He was none too pleased and tried to speak to me, his anger apparent even though my English was poor then. I gave Dorothy my address and returned to camp, as always.

I thought that was the end of it. Two days later, a parcel arrived with chocolates, cigarettes, and money to lure me back to London for the weekend. With our measly pay, I couldn't say no. Beggars can't be choosers. I visited the girl on Sunday, just for an hour, before returning to camp. This routine continued while we idled at camp, unsure of our next orders.

One Thursday, they roused us early and instructed us to don our navy-blue uniforms for a lineup at eleven. We assembled, not knowing what awaited us. A group of high-ranking officers approached, led by General Charles de Gaulle himself. He was there to inspect and commend what remained of the third battalion, second company of marines. We presented arms and he presented us with the Cross of Lorraine, with his signature inscribed on each one. When he reached me, he asked, "How old are you, mon petit?"

"Seventeen," I replied.

"Very well, my son," he nodded.

The Free French provisional government in London gave us three options. Stay with the Free French Forces. Join the Merchant Navy. Or be repatriated to South America. Finally, I saw a chance to chase my dream. I wanted to become a bullfighter in Mexico. Mariano and I opted for repatriation. In Mexico, they cherished Spanish traditions, just as they did across other Spanish-speaking lands. My friend Larrauro landed a job with the Latin American division of the BBC in London. We all headed to London at discharge. Half the boys took rooms at the Royal Hotel. The rest took rooms at the Hills Hotel. Mariano and I waited for our demobilization papers and visas for Colombia.

Our buses pulled up to the Hills Hotel. A place as silent as a mortuary. Half-dead souls and old ladies populated it. They knitted through the night. The atmosphere was heavy and depressing. We decided to lighten the mood. Several girls were there, and they were attractive. We cleared the salon of tables and chairs. We transformed it into a makeshift dance hall. The English guests were reserved and set in their ways. They were shocked at first. Soon they joined in. They danced with us until dawn each night. German bombs fell not too far off. A grim reminder of the war. We joked that if death were to find us, better to meet it in the embrace of a beautiful girl.

My room turned into a harem. Girls visited constantly, including the redhead Dorothy from Hammersmith Palais. The Free French Government covered our hotel stay. They provided a modest stipend. I had no choice and accepted the pocket money from Dorothy, and I was honest with her about my plans to leave for Colombia. Plans that didn't include her. My commitment to learning English was minimal. I was bound for a Spanish-speaking country. Dorothy turned to an English-Spanish dictionary to communicate with me. Over time, I recognized her genuine affection and my own selfishness.

Franco held Spain tight and nobody wanted to acknowledge the Spanish government. This led to delays in our visas to Colombia. Being Spanish was like having leprosy back then. For years, Spain suffered under a monarchy. The king hunted and travelled while the people starved. They were jobless and persecuted. Then the Second Republic brought hope. A brief period of renewal before capitalists incited a civil war. The people fought for the Republic. Anyone defending their rights risked being labelled a communist. A term many hardly understood.

The captain laid out the options again. Mariano and I had to choose. We could return to the Free French Forces or sign up with the Merchant Navy. They had to rush our demobilization papers now. The provisional French government outfitted us in suits that came from Savile Row. They were made by the finest tailors in England but with the war was on fabric was scarce. My jacket was short. It was so short it looked like a matador's outfit, not a Savile Row suit. I must have looked ridiculous. Mariano had become the peacemaker now. We planned our exit from England. We tried the shipping companies for a berth. My English was poor, so poor I asked for a 'chip' instead of a 'ship.' They directed me to fish and chip shops instead. Eventually we secured a spot and got passage on a Belgian vessel.

Mariano signed on as a trimmer. I signed on as a deck boy. Our demobilization papers were still pending and without them, we couldn't board. Eventually we managed to get

Mariano's papers sorted. We went to the commanding officer of the French forces. Mine weren't ready and he had to leave without me. The ship was docked in Liverpool. We took the train from London and at the station, tough Mariano cried like a child. I cried too. I didn't care what anyone thought. Six days after the ship left Liverpool, it was torpedoed. Everyone on board died. Mariano died too. I was lucky. My papers finally arrived. I signed onto a Greek ship as an assistant cook. Before leaving, I told Dorothy something. "Wait for me. We'll marry when I return."

The ship was probably an old piece Onassis picked up from a museum. It had a decent crew, but I spoke little English. They knew no French or Spanish. Communication would be tough. We moored outside London. We were short three crew members. My shifts ran from five in the morning till eight at night. A grueling schedule. It had me slaving in the galley like Cinderella. I hated it. I was determined not to stay aboard long. The chief engineer was a decent man. He woke me each morning with a cup of tea and an orange.

Onc afternoon, I was taking in some fresh air on deck. A motorboat approached with the three crewmen we were missing. I watched to see who they were. To my surprise, I recognized them. They were the South Americans who had fought with me in the French forces. Mountains can't meet. People can. Now I wasn't alone after all. We set out from London for Scotland. We were joining a convoy heading back to the United States. It was meant to be a large convoy. There were 165 ships. Only 44 made it. The newspapers called it one of the Allies' greatest losses of the war. Our ship was old. It was barely managing 7 knots. The newer American Liberty ships could do 14 knots. After we passed Ireland, we lost the rest of the convoy. The Germans likely didn't bother with us. They figured our slow ship wasn't worth a torpedo.

Fourteen days later, we made it to Halifax, Nova Scotia. We docked at three in the afternoon. My mates went ashore to have fun. I was stuck in the kitchen. I was the ship's Cinderella. But that day, I finished early and went ashore in the suit the Free French had given me. It was laughable. As I headed down the gangway the chief engineer asked to join me. I agreed. We stopped in front of a tailor's shop. A fine navy-blue suit was displayed in the window. "Try it on," he urged. "Why? I'm not buying," I protested. He insisted. Inside, the double-breasted suit fit perfectly. He even had me try on a raincoat and then shoes. I tired of it. I had no money to spend. Finally, I told him I was off to the cinema. He returned to the ship. After watching a movie, I went back to find my cabin filled with surprises. Two suits. Half a dozen shirts. Underwear. A raincoat. Three pairs of expensive shoes. All gifts from him. My heart swelled with gratitude.

6

A MAN AT SEA

I had plans to go to Mexico. Jumping ship in Halifax wasn't wise, so I resigned to return to England and wait for another chance. Dorothy and her family had been kind. I bought them a small gift. I had put aside any thoughts of marriage. I hadn't received a single letter from her while away. Marriage was not really in my plans. While we waited for a convoy, the chief engineer bought me two leather jackets and a silk one from a vendor beside our ship.

We picked up the convoy back to England and lost it again, crossing the Atlantic alone. It was harrowing. Debris from torpedoed ships floated past. A grim sight. Yet we made it. We docked at Convoy Wharf along the Thames on a Saturday afternoon. There, I found a bundle of letters from Dorothy. Twelve in total. In one, she wrote of going to bed at seven each night, waiting for me. The war had delayed their delivery. I hurried over to her place with the gifts. She was just getting ready for bed and burst into tears when she saw me. Since leaving Spain, I hadn't written home. She had written to my parents, asking for permission for us to marry. My father consented, perhaps hoping it would settle me.

There wasn't much to do except agree. I proposed we marry the next Monday, Easter.

The ship's captain agreed to be my best man. I told the chief engineer. He broke down.

"After all I've done for you," he said. "And you're leaving me."

I shared this with a South American crewmate. He laughed.

"You didn't know?" he said. "He's fallen for you."

I was taken aback. Nothing inappropriate had passed between us. I respected him greatly for that. The natural order was clear. I preferred it that way.

I had always been with women since I was young, and I wasn't about to change that. There's a story from my time in London that seems humorous now, but it wasn't then. At the Hills Hotel, where I sometimes stayed, there was an English lady with a nine-year-old son. The boy was paralysed from the waist up. He was teaching me English. His mother worked all day for the navy, leaving him alone in the hotel, so I felt sorry for him.

One day I offered to take him to the movies. His mother was grateful, and the next day we went.

During the film the boy signaled he needed the restroom. In the bathroom he couldn't manage his zipper because of his paralysis, and I helped him. A sailor walked in and misunderstood the situation. He thought I was harming the boy and yelled in English. I yelled back in Spanish. We nearly came to blows.

The police arrived, but they couldn't understand me either, and tensions rose because they thought I was a child molester. I was furious, trying to explain, when a young man from Gibraltar stepped in. He spoke both Spanish and English and clarified everything. The police apologised once they realized their mistake, but it was already too much for me. Everyone was shaking hands, apologizing, the typical Anglo-Saxon way—hurt first, then apologize. After that, I vowed never to help anyone again. But you can't change who you are, as you'll see later in my story.

I left the ship with £190, a small fortune in those days, enough for a small car. My wedding had three ship captains in attendance, my own captain as my best man. We married, and though I've seen my share of horrors at sea, I was neither brave nor a coward. I decided to stay in England for a while.

In wartime, everyone did their part, and I enrolled in a welding course, thinking the skill might prove useful. Not far from London, in Hounslow, was a training school filled with beautiful English girls learning trades before heading to wartime factory jobs. Among them, I imagined myself a Valentino, enjoying the company of many friendly and lovely girls. My wife saw things differently. Her love turned to hate and jealousy, and my life became unbearable.

After completing my training, I worked in a factory making landing crafts and tanks. The job paid well, and I was responsible and respected for my work. At work, I was content. At home was another story. My wife accused me nightly of being with every woman in London. Maybe she had her reasons, but I was not that man. I came home each evening to find my clothes hidden, her way of keeping me in. We lived with her mother and family. Kind though my mother-in-law was kind, the house felt like a prison. She supported her daughter, as expected, yet I knew she liked me. When I went to work, I felt free. Unable to endure that life any longer, I decided to return to sea, preferring the dangers there to the confinement at home. I told my wife I needed my freedom, not a divorce. Despite her promises to change, my mind was set on leaving.

Leaving the job was complicated. It was crucial work during the war. I told my manager I was quitting, but he objected. We ended up before a labour exchange judge, who ruled against me because I was an essential worker. I had another plan, however. The next day, I deliberately exposed my eyes to the welding glare without a mask. My eyes watered painfully, and a doctor declared me unfit for welding. With medical proof, they had to let me go. Though I suffered for days, it was worth it.

A week later, I was in Liverpool, hunting for a ship. Liverpool was a haven of women, and I revelled in their company like a sultan. At a sailors' home, I met another Spaniard looking for a ship. He was seasoned; I barely knew the sea. Yet we struck a friendship, and he suggested we ship out together. At the shipping office, there was a spot for two first-class seamen. The Spaniard urged me to join as an able seaman, but I knew nothing of ships. My only ship job having been as a galley boy. He promised to teach me and after a long talk, he persuaded me. I signed on as an able seaman.

The ship I boarded was under no specific flag that I care to mention, as it was filled with more Nazis than you'd find in Germany itself. It was docked in the Manchester Canal, a 36-mile stretch linking Manchester to the Irish Sea. The shipping company provided us with fares and a letter of introduction to the captain. The canal was crowded with ships of various nationalities, many manned by foreigners. My mate and I walked the wharf with our suitcases. After searching for half an hour, we discovered our ship was the largest one there. We climbed aboard and handed the letter to the chief mate, who straightaway told us to stow our gear and get to work. So far, so good! I followed my Spanish mate's lead, mimicking his actions. Around five in the afternoon, the captain strode onto the bridge with a microphone and bellowed, "Mora, come up to the bridge." He wanted me to pilot the ship out to sea. The shock nearly killed me. My name echoing in such a critical command sent shivers through me. My legs trembled like leaves, and I turned as pale as a ghost.

I had never set foot in a wheelhouse, much less steered a ship. How was I supposed to take that behemoth out to sea? I wanted to flee, run all the way back to London. But it was too late. I couldn't tell the captain I wasn't a seaman. They would've jailed me for six months for falsifying my role. Yet, recalling my father's words—that the world was not made for cowards—I found the courage to step up to the bridge and take the wheel. Terrified, with no time even to pray, I somehow managed to guide the ship out to sea, risking the lives of 43 men. After two hours, when I was relieved, I went down and kissed the deck, much like Columbus must have when he sighted land after his long, dangerous voyage. My mate hadn't moved from his spot, half-expecting a disaster, but he was proud, and so was I.

The crew on this ship was different from any before—mostly Nazis and fascists. I couldn't fathom why the British had let them land. Among them was a reserved English fireman, unkempt and solitary, and a constantly drunk French fireman. Shortly after we set sail, the captain asked me to fill in at the officer's mess since immigration issues had prevented the usual boy from signing on. I agreed, thinking it temporary. But I regretted it, surrounded by men who had fought for Franco and boasted that Germany would win the war. So, I waged a quiet rebellion. The chief steward allocated three eggs per man for breakfast. I gave them only one each, hoarding the rest. I also pilfered soap and any supplies I could carry—butter, marmalade. I wouldn't let these men eat well while my friends and their families suffered in England. Many times, the officers complained about the food. I told them, "We are at war. Millions are starving. You're lucky to get anything at all." If they knew the truth about how I was skimming their portions, I'd likely end up at the bottom of the sea.

In one of the rooms on the ship there was a long table where the crew played poker nightly for cigarettes. An Argentinian sailor among us never smoked but played with skill. He asked me to supply his cigarettes, promising to win on my behalf. Each night, I handed him cartons. By morning, my cabin overflowed with his winnings. Two days before Newfoundland, I had crammed four cartons of food and three of cigarettes into my cabin. The officers grew suspicious and irate about their meals. I couldn't leave my fate to chance. So, I confronted the captain. I'd sign on for temporary mess duty, not the entire voyage. He didn't budge. "You can't refuse duty," he said. I challenged him and we argued. Refusing duty at sea during wartime meant mutiny— punishable by imprisonment or death. Instead of shooting me, the captain confined me to my cabin.

In Newfoundland, they court-martialled me. Twelve British Marines boarded with a high-ranking officer. We gathered in the salon, a large table between us. The British officer took one end, the ship's captain the other. I sat in the middle, ringed by marines. The inquiry started. The British officer glared directly at me.

"The captain says you refused duties at sea," he said. "Is that the truth?

In my broken English I said, "Yes, it's true. I refused duties because I signed on as able seaman, not to be a mess boy the whole trip."

The British officer asked if this was correct. The captain admitted it but argued, "He is not a seaman now."

Frustrated, I shot back, "Then who took the ship out of the Manchester Canal?"

The captain didn't answer.

"I did," I said.

The British officer was now visibly annoyed. He pointed at the captain.

"If he took the ship out, treat him as a seaman on his return to England.'

And he turned to me while pointed at the ship's captain.

"If he causes any trouble, report it. He could lose his rank. I'm tired of foreign captains bending maritime law."

The inquiry ended swiftly!

7

THE SHIP THAT NEVER RETURNED

Back at the helm, I steered with more confidence. We headed from St. John, Newfoundland's capital, to a small village to load paper. The approach was tricky. Rocks everywhere. No one could guide you through. We navigated by following lights. Despite this, the captain entrusted me to pilot our large ship into the harbor. I took the challenge head-on. With every successful manoeuvre, even the captain couldn't hide his relief. I steered, threading through hazards with newfound skill.

I thought to myself, "You are doing better than the great Manolete."

The village was mostly filled with Canadian troops. Despite the odds, I met a pretty girl who took me to her eerie house that seemed straight out of a horror film. We spent a couple of hours together before she had to leave. Confused and late at night, I stayed in bed. Moments later, her mother joined me and explained her daughter was married to a Canadian soldier and had to meet him. Soon after, I learned her husband came to know about me. For my safety, I stayed on board while the ship was being loaded. The local mood was unforgiving—they'd rather shoot first and ask questions later.

Once loaded, we joined another American convoy. The Liberty ships raced ahead, and we struggled to keep up. At night thick fog rolled in and obscured everything. By morning the fog had cleared.

We were alone.

The radio from Canada crackled with orders for the captain: proceed to England or risk losing rank. Desperate to keep his stripes, the captain risked our lives. He pushed through the perilous Atlantic. The return to England was harrowing, isolated in the vast ocean, an easy target. Perhaps the Germans spared us, deeming our old vessel unworthy of their torpedoes. Little did they know. Beneath the rolls of paper on the deck, the hold was packed with tanks and airplanes.

As we neared England, the captain kept praising me

"You're the best sailor we have on board," he said.

If only he knew the truth. He wanted me to stay, but I was set on leaving.

"Just pay me off as soon as we reach London," I told him curtly.

Once we berthed, I had arranged via telegram for my brother-in-law to meet me with his truck. I was smuggling three big boxes of cigarettes and four cases of food, winnings from the Argentinian sailor's poker games. Bribing English customs was nearly impossible back then, and I worried about getting the cigarettes ashore. But as we approached London, the Germans began dropping V2 bombs over the city. Chaos reigned thinning the docks. Just my brother-in-law waiting with his truck. We loaded the contraband quickly and drove off before anyone noticed.

Returning to the ship later to settle my affairs, I found the wharf swarming with police. They boarded and soon emerged with the French fireman in handcuffs and the English fireman following behind, caught in some misdeed. The distraction they caused was the last bit of luck I needed. The captain explained it all. The Frenchman, always drunk, turned out to be a spy. The quiet English fireman was a British Secret Service agent. They had been watching him for a long time, suspecting he was signalling the Germans at sea. I had felt sorry for them, but I was fooled. Who would have guessed that these two apparent bums were a spy and a secret agent?

In London, they paid me nearly £400! My wife was expecting, so I chose to stay and see if she could trust me again, though I couldn't fault her if she didn't. I landed a job at a tank factory and bought a racing bicycle. After work, I'd ride for miles. Some people admire beautiful pictures or flowers. I admired beautiful women.

One day, after a long ride, I stopped in a park to rest. A stunning blonde with blue eyes sat next to me. She too had a bike. We struck up a conversation, and she invited me to her place. That was the end of peace. She ignited a war between my wife and me.

I didn't get home until two in the morning. My wife was furious, demanding to know where I had been. I told her I'd been riding and ended up in a place called Reading. She didn't buy it

The next day I came home to change after work. My wife greeted me at the door. "Close your eyes," she said. When I opened them, there was a lady's bike in front of me.

"What's this for?"

"To go out riding with you."

I told her she couldn't come. It wouldn't look right with my friends. She ignored me, followed as I dressed and took off on my bike. I was faster, but at a crossroads I dodged a car by sprinting hard on the pedals. She couldn't stop in time. She got thrown through the air like a ragdoll. She was pregnant.

That was the start of real trouble. I couldn't handle this life anymore. I shipped out again.

In Liverpool, I met three South American seamen. Now as a qualified able seaman, finding a ship was no trouble, and we shipped out together. The ship was bound for the United States, from where I planned to reach Mexico to pursue my dream of becoming a bullfighter. Each of us had different plans.

Six days out from Liverpool, the German air force attacked. A bomb struck the bow. The ship began taking on water badly. We struggled for ten hours to save her, but she was sinking fast, and the captain ordered us to abandon ship. We took to the lifeboat, drifting at sea for four hours until the American Coast Guard rescued us and brought us to New York.

There I received a letter from my wife announcing the birth of our son. The bullfighting dream felt different now. All I wanted was to return to England and settle down. But how? We had lost the ship, and I needed to find a way back. In New York, we were paid off with $1,500—to make up for lost property among other things. With that money, we bought clothes and enjoyed ourselves, uncertain of what the future held.

There was a Greek seaman on that ship who never set foot on shore, his belt and suitcase stuffed with pound notes—over 20,000 pounds saved in 17 years. So, when the captain ordered us to abandon ship, he was among the first in the lifeboat. Yet he jumped out to retrieve a suitcase filled with dirty clothes from his cabin and went down with the ship. After that, we threw caution to the wind in New York, splurging on clothes and buying a second-hand car to tour the city and its surrounds. We were having a good time. After witnessing the horrors of war, who felt like saving money?

In New York, we each spent $400 on clothes. We hit the best nightclubs and lived large. Soon our funds ran dry. Desperate for work, we looked for another ship. I was eager to return to England to see my son, but there were no direct ships available. Reluctantly, the four of us signed on with a Swedish ship.

If you sign on with a foreign vessel, the company must repatriate you to the country where you enlisted. I was desperate to return to England. I would have gone through hell to get back. I joined the ship planning to jump ship as soon as we reached England. Sweden was neutral during the war, allowing its ships access to nearly any part of the world.

We were aboard a Red Cross ship, and our first destination was Greece, occupied by the Germans. The three South Americans and I, all from neutral countries, became hesitant as we went ashore, fearing interrogation. But it was too late to turn back. Upon arrival, surprisingly, the Germans issued us passes without questions, allowing us some freedom. During our time in Greece, we managed to cause trouble for the Germans, so in the last few days we had to remain on board. It was too risky to venture out.

From Greece, we headed to the Soviet Union. The people there were friendly and kind but constantly asked us when the Allies would open a second front. Russian soldiers were dying in vast numbers. We explained that we were not politicians, yet they treated us well despite our unhelpful answers.

In that place, I met a wonderful girl. I might have jumped ship for her, but I needed to see my son in England. The wages were excellent aboard, and I hadn't spent much, so when we reached England, I told the captain my wife was ill.

He kindly paid me off, but I regretted leaving the ship. She
was bound for South America next, and from there I could
have made it to Mexico to chase my bullfighting dreams. But
it was too late. I belonged to my son now, a boy I'd never
seen. I doubted I'd find a ship like that again—a ship more
like a passenger liner, safe from the dark and torpedoes.

8

TRADING IN SHADOWS

Landing in London with a full pocket, I was on my way to meet my son for the first time. Riding the bus home, I couldn't stop thinking. If I went back to sea, maybe I wouldn't see him again. I might not be so lucky next time. I'd done enough for victory. At home, I told my wife about my fears, and we promised each other fidelity. I couldn't keep that promise.

I was a boilermaker in London now and we were content. How long would this happiness last? I loved my son dearly and though I could no longer become a bullfighter. I dreamed he might and devoted all my time to him. Soon my wife was pregnant again. With the birth of another boy, it seemed my days at sea were truly over. I was a good father. I was a faithful husband. Yet inside me, two men fought: the saint and the sinner.

We were happy, and I hoped that one of my boys would become a bullfighter. I played with them charge like a bull using a coat hanger. The older one scared easily and didn't want to play. The younger one never blinked. This courage made me believe he was destined for the ring. My wife disagreed and was determined he would be a doctor. Despite this, I became a good husband. I came home every night. I brought my wages to my wife. I played with my sons. I avoided going out alone because I didn't trust myself. I surprised myself.

They were showing a film I wanted to see In one of the theatres in London. When I got home from work, I invited my wife to join me. She declined and urged me to go alone. I said I wouldn't go without her, but she persuaded me to go by myself. The theatre was just around the corner. It was the first time in months I'd gone out alone. I was enjoying the film until an attractive girl took the seat next to me. From that moment, I couldn't follow the movie. I couldn't take my eyes off her. She offered me a cigarette, and we started chatting. We struck up a friendship before the film ended.

After the movie, I walked her home and asked why she was alone. "I don't have a boyfriend, or other friends," she said. That was all the invitation I needed. She was lovely and I felt for her loneliness, so I played along. "I don't have a girlfriend either," I said. "Maybe we could be friends?" I was married with two kids, living not far from where she was. There I was, playing Valentino, knowing well the part I should not have taken.

I came home at four in the morning, igniting yet another civil war with my wife. The next day, I visited the girl from the cinema. Her mother answered the door. She looked at me and smiled. "She's been singing this morning," she said. "I haven't heard her sing in two years." The mother told me other things. Her daughter had been lonely. Very lonely. She had talked of ending it all. I did my best to cheer her up and kept visiting. As I did, I became more entangled. My marriage teetered on the brink. I thought about my wife at home. I thought about my two boys. I thought about this girl who sang now because I visited her. I couldn't stop visiting and I couldn't keep visiting. I went to Liverpool and signed onto a ship.

It was an old Greek ship owned by Onassis, so decrepit it belonged in a museum rather than on the seas. During wartime, it was deemed sufficient. That's how shipowners amassed their fortunes. The ship took me everywhere, finally bringing me to Canada. It offered good money for those who lived long enough to enjoy it. But Henry Morgan would have been ashamed. And Francis Drake would have spat. This old tramp of a ship was loaded to the brim with planes and tanks for England. Perilous cargo.

After loading, we were ordered to wait on the high seas for an American convoy heading to England. Once again, the American ships were too fast for us. Three days out of Canada, we lost them. We received a signal that German forces were just two hours away. The captain radioed Navy headquarters about losing the convoy. The blunt reply came: "Proceed or else." With no escort, we had no choice and braved the Atlantic alone. We counted each hour, expecting to be hit at any moment. Our cargo was dangerous. Planes and tanks visible for miles. The days passed slowly. Each night we watched for submarines. Each morning we were still afloat. The crew didn't talk much.

We crossed the Atlantic and as soon as I saw the English coast, I requested to be paid off. Upon arrival, they told us no one could leave the ship. By six o'clock that evening, we were at sea again, heading for Scotland. We didn't know our destination from there. Then we saw hundreds of ships massed together. It was for the invasion of France. There was nothing to be done about it. Besides, none of us had seen anything like this before. We ferried troops and supplies across the Channel for weeks. The ship made crossing after crossing and we watched the war from the water.

After returning to England, I was finally paid off. I returned to my wife and children and witnessed the end of World War II in Europe. It dawned on me then how the capitalist world finds ample funds for war but not for peace. During the war, there was plenty of money and work. Peace brought unemployment, hunger, and misery. Factories shut down. Thousands of soldiers returned home to no jobs. What, then, was the point of fighting for your country?

For two months I was on the dole. It felt degrading. I searched everywhere for work but eventually had to return to sea. I secured a position as a bosun, managing deckhands on a Panamanian ship running between London and Finland. The pay was excellent. After years of fighting for others, it was time to fight for myself and think about earning more money.

Post-war Germany was in a bad state and people were desperate. As we headed for Finland, we picked up a German pilot to navigate the Kiel Canal. The pilot came aboard wearing an old coat with gold rings in his pockets. He wanted cigarettes so I gave him some and he gave me the rings. Each time we passed through the canal, I traded. I came back loaded with cigarettes and other goods.

We docked in Finland at a place called Mäntyluoto. There were many women with blonde hair and blue eyes, working as labourers. Some came to the ship often to my cabin. There was a girl, Elsa, from a nearby village called Viglaba. She'd visit me one day, and I'd visit her the next. She spoke English and as mine improved, we got along well.

One day, I took the train to visit Elsa when another striking girl sat opposite me. Her name was Helmi, and I offered her an American cigarette. We became friendly though she only spoke Finnish. She gestured for me to come with her, and I did. She lived five stops from Elsa's and though barely spoke English, we understood each other well enough.

We reached Helmi's station where her mother and two other girls awaited us with vodka. At Helmi's house, another waiting. Inside, the setup was simple: a bed, a kitchen, and a bathroom, all in one large room. They all sat on the floor, drinking vodka like water. I wasn't there to drink and had travelled twenty miles for another reason.

By ten in the evening, I bluntly told Helmi, "I came here to sleep with you."

She seemed to understand me and simply said, "Get into bed."

I gestured with a frown at the presence of the other women.

With candid reassurance she simply said, "It is okay."

So, I said, "If you don't care, I don't care either," and got into bed though it didn't feel quite right.

Moments later, she slipped into bed too, and we made love in front of everyone. Surprisingly, her mother joined us in bed half an hour later, and I found myself compelled to extend my affections to her as well. The situation escalated quickly; all the women were desirable but they were drunk. The small bed couldn't hold everyone, so they ended up sleeping on the floor. At around two in the morning, tears began to flow. Emotions ran high. By six, there was a knock on the door.

Elsa whispered, "That's my husband."

I was trapped.

The husband entered the room while I was still in bed with his wife. He seemed unfazed, shrugging and putting down more bottles of vodka to the mix. Half an hour later, the room filled with tears and drunken sorrow. I couldn't stand it any longer. I dressed quickly and made my way to the station, desperate to escape.

At the station, I tried to communicate in English, French, and Spanish, asking for the train to Mäntyluoto. The station master didn't understand a word. Worried about boarding the wrong train and accidentally heading toward the Soviet Union, I left the station in frustration. Outside, I spotted a large sign pointing the way to Mäntyluoto. Walking was the safer option, so I set off on foot back to the ship, seeking the familiarity and relative safety of my berth aboard.

The Finnish countryside is a vast forest, and in the summer, the mosquitoes were thick. With the road empty, they swarmed me all the way back to the ship. I can't recall how long the walk took, but I arrived back at the ship around nine at night, my face and eyes swollen from the bites. I spent the next two days in bed, suffering from chills and a fever. On the third day, the fever broke. I got up and went back to work.

After the Second World War, coffee was scarce in Finland. It fetched high prices. One day at the wharf in Mäntyluoto, a man approached me. We talked. He asked about the ship, where we'd been. Then he said, "Coffee is worth a lot here". He paused. "If you bring me any amount of coffee, I'll pay in whatever currency you choose."

I also discovered that export-quality radios were inexpensively available in Finland. This prompted me to plan for our next trip. While we were unloading, the captain ordered us to proceed to Luebeck in Germany. It proved to be another lucrative market. There, ten cartons of cigarettes could buy a Leica camera worth several hundred pounds. I managed to get two cameras for twenty cartons. In London, a 20-kilo sack of coffee was 10 pounds. In Finland, they paid 1500 markkas per kilo. The bank offering 750 markkas for one English pound, so the profit margin was substantial.

All I had to do was arrange for coffee to be delivered to our ship in London, and in Finland, they would come aboard to unload it. There was nothing left for me to do. I just collected the money. My cabin, along with other parts of the ship, was filled with sacks of coffee.

My contact in Germany was a seasoned black-marketeer. With Germany added to our trading route, I was set to make substantial profits. Everyone on the ship was involved in the black market, from the captain down to the deck boy. Cigarettes had become more valuable than cash. Crew members preferred their wages in tobacco over pound notes. Given the choice, I too opted to be paid in cigarettes. My profits soared. I then asked the German to pay me in jewellery instead of cameras. The cameras were bulky and harder to sell. I never inquired where he got his jewellery. I wasn't wise to ask too many questions under those circumstances.

9

PAYING THE DEVIL HIS DUE

Back in London, I spent my days with my boys and my nights at high-end nightclubs, mingling with the influential. One night, I was introduced to a well-spoken man, Johnny Rice. He had a big stature in the London underworld, as it turned out. He had served in the International Brigades, the volunteer army formed by the Communist International to support the Second Spanish Republic. He took a liking to me. He was a dapper criminal, a gentleman gangster. Owning a mansion outside London, several cars, a yacht, and more, he was, in essence, the Padrino, a godfather of the underworld. After grilling me on my background and comings-and-goings, he said, "Any time you need me, don't hesitate to call." It was a comforting offer. Life was surely unpredictable.

Back then, I had no reason to take up his offer. In London, I had a contact with a fence who would buy the jewellery from me as soon as the ship docked. No questions asked. All transactions were handled on board, sparing me the risk of carrying hot property around. There were no receipts for the jewellery, I suspected they were stolen. Despite the considerable profits, I found myself spending as quickly as I earned. After ten voyages, the money had vanished as fast as it came. It evaporated. My lavish lifestyle consumed all of it. You pay dearly for your desires. The ship was then ordered to the Pacific Ocean. It was a journey I couldn't join. God only knew when it would return, and I wanted to stay close to my sons.

Paid off in London, the money soon ran out. I had grown accustomed to the good life. Endless months passed as my wife and I grew more estranged. I didn't want a divorce because of my sons. Truth be told, she was not to blame for our troubles.

Yet again, I found myself jobless in England. Jobs were scarce and working conditions were dismal. Almost reminiscent of the bleakness under Franco's Spain. I wondered why so many had died in World War II only for us to end up like this. Factories were shutting down. Those with jobs were at the mercy of their employers' whims. It was a life I couldn't stomach. As my relationship with my wife deteriorated further, it became clear I couldn't stay. I didn't blame her for wanting distance. It was time to find a new place to live.

Things were so dire that I couldn't even pay the rent. The landlord had come looking for me twice that week. I needed money and I needed it fast. As a last resort, I thought of my new acquaintance. The godfather. The London underworld figure I had met months before in a nightclub. He had given me his card and told me to call if I ever needed anything. I hesitated. I knew what kind of man he was. I knew what working for him might mean. But I thought I had no choice.

I found him at his usual spot, in a private club in Soho. When he saw me, his face changed. Once, I had worn tailored suits. Now I stood before him poorly dressed and unshaven:

shirt wrinkled, shoes scuffed. He probably pitied me and remarked, "By the looks of it, you haven't fared well."

I admitted, "Yes, that's why I'm here."

"Well," he said, "let's cut to the chase. I might have work for you on my payroll. But remember, any hint of treachery, and you'll pay dearly. Understand?"

"Yes," I replied, hiding my nerves about what I was stepping into.

He pulled out his wallet and handed me 200 pounds, declaring, "That's your weekly wage from now on, and here's another 200 pounds to buy some decent clothes." He instructed me to meet him the next day to discuss what I had to do for him.

In those days, 200 pounds a week was a fortune. Possibly more than the Prime Minister made, I thought. What would I have to do to earn this? With the money, I first had a decent meal. I paid the weeks of overdue rent that my landlord had been chasing. With the remaining cash, I bought clothes.

The next day, I learned my role. Since I had no police record, I was to visit specific spots in London to collect money. Those who didn't pay were to be reported to him. His clients feared him; collection was typically hassle-free. The pay was excellent. I stayed with him for months, but I despised the work. Despite Johnny Rice's elegant appearance and manner, he was just a standover man, a racketeer living off the backs of prostitutes and the powerless. Working for him made me just as corrupt.

At the time, London was caught in a gang war. Rivals clashed over territory and trade. Many ending up in the mortuary. I was determined not to be one of them - not for 200 pounds. I wasn't willing to spend my life in jail just to line his pockets. After four months, I decided to quit. I knew the decision was perilous. Betraying him was out of the question. Nobody just walked away from his gang, especially for someone like me who knew too much about his operations across London. The safest exit strategy seemed to be leaving the country.

I only needed to collect money on Fridays. That left most of my week free. Staying could mean a dire fate. I wasn't willing to die for wealth gained through crime. By Monday, I had saved enough money and made my way to a seaport in Hull.

There, a modern pirate ship under the Panamanian flag was docking. I heard they needed an able seaman. I met with the captain and got the job. He provided a letter for the immigration department, and soon, I had permission to leave the country. Back on board, I chatted with a crew member who revealed our mission. We were transporting Jews from Marseille to Haifa in what was then Palestine under British protection. The British navy was patrolling the Mediterranean to prevent Jewish landings. Curious, I asked an officer how England could justify such actions. "Politics, my son," he shrugged. We set sail. Our next stop was Gibraltar. We arrived on a Friday with plans to depart the following Monday. I looked forward to few days of pleasure in Gibraltar.

As usual, I spent the evening at a nightclub. I enjoyed myself until around 2 o'clock in the morning when I decided to head back to the ship. It was a beautiful night. The sea air filling my lungs as I walked. I was lost in thought about the mess my life had become and how to escape it. Suddenly I heard a woman cry for help. I was there, so I went to investigate. I found a man striking a woman. I intervened, stepping between them and telling him to leave her alone. He turned to me and said, "Perhaps you'd like to take over her part?" Then he launched into an attack.

We fought. He swung at me and I swung back, grappling on the footpath. As I was beginning to lose, something struck head. A sharp blow knocked me unconscious. Down on the footpath, everything went dark. When I came to, the police had arrived and took me to the hospital. There, I learned that a prostitute had struck me on the head with the heel of her shoe. The man was her pimp. Their argument had been a ruse to rob me. They took all my money. That painful lesson taught me never to interfere again. When you're born stupid, you die stupid. I never seemed to learn.

After Gibraltar, we headed to Marseille to begin loading what some called human cargo, destined for Haifa, Palestine. It was heard to see the suffering of these people. The ship was crammed with poor Jews. They slept on the deck and in every available space. For centuries, Jews have faced persecution from the Christian world. I never understood this. Jesus of Nazareth was himself a Jew. The persecution seemed driven more by politics than religion. Many said they cared too much about money. But without money, they could not survive. I did what I could to help them settle. We often risked breaking through the British blockade to reach Haifa. Getting caught would have meant long prison sentences for all of us. But it was a risk worth taking.

The pay was tempting, but the principle behind it mattered more. I had made several trips on that ship. Then the conflict in Palestine escalated. British soldiers were being targeted in Palestine. I started to see it differently. I had moved to England as a young boy. My friends were English. My children were English. If I kept helping the Jews in Palestine, I was betraying my own. It felt as if I were attacking those soldiers myself. I've made many mistakes in my life. But being a traitor was not one I would add to that list. I asked to be paid off in Marseille.

I stayed in Marseille for a while, living by the waterfront, and taking any work that came my way. But I kept thinking about England. In my dreams, I heard my children's voices.

They asked when I would return. I couldn't find peace. I couldn't sleep soundly. One night, I decided to go back. I stowed away on a ship bound for London. The distance was short. I didn't tell the captain and hid in a lifeboat. I stayed there until we docked in London. No one knew I had returned.

I tried to start over. I looked for work. I tried to see my wife and children. But it was too late. My wife's love for me had faded and I couldn't blame her. There I was again, drifting through the streets of London, trying to live carefree. But thoughts of the gangster haunted me. What would he do if he found me? In Marseille, I had thought about joining the Foreign Legion. But the thought of my children held me back. I longed to see them. I couldn't even afford to buy them chocolate. No matter how hard I tried, I couldn't find work.

Driven to desperation one night, I committed my first crime with my brother-in-law. It was petty burglary. We stole small things. But everyone must start somewhere. Once again, I was back in the fast lane. This time, I worked for myself. I lived in Maida Vale. It was a wealthy area with large Victorian houses. The houses were worth robbing. My brother-in-law and I did well for a while, but my past caught up with me.

Johnny Rice, the gentleman gangster, learned I was back in London and sought revenge. He tipped off the police. The police thought I had done more than I had charging me for burglaries across London. I was arrested and brought me before a judge. He gave me six months in prison and said I should be deported.

My time in prison wasn't as bad as expected. I became something of a star prisoner. Being a first-timer, I had certain privileges. I could wear civilian clothes sometimes. One hot day, I left my leather jacket in my cell during exercise time. When I returned, it was gone. I went to the prison chief and told him, "Sir, someone stole my jacket." He looked me over from head to toe and said deadpan, "Well, my son, this place is full of crooks."

Prison had a rule. After thirteen weeks, they paid three pennies and a quarter packet of tobacco. A packet cost a shilling. Twelve pennies to a shilling. The next tobacco ration came three weeks later. Another week for paper and matches. By the time prisoners had everything they needed to smoke, they got out!

I was assigned to work in the yard breaking rocks. The rocks were for prison construction; gravel for pathways. To pass the hours, I worked faster than others. I broke more stones. The prison governor noticed during his rounds and called me a good worker. That led to my transfer to the farm prison party. Working on the farm meant leaving early in the morning and returning late in the afternoon. The farm was distant from the prison and was a welcome change from breaking rocks.

Work at the farm sometimes felt like a holiday. At lunch, we swam in the nearby river. Land army girls working close by would bring cigarettes to the river. Other times, we sat by the road and begged passing cars for cigarettes. Drivers often tossed a pack to us in our prison uniforms. I distributed the cigarettes among the prisoners. That made me popular.

But prison discipline was strict. The wardens were tough. There was one warden known as The Terror. His real name was Rita. He had been a sergeant in the army and ran a tight ship. Inside the prison, he was merciless. Outside, he was surprisingly personable. One day, I asked him, "How come you're nice out here, but inside you're The Terror?"

He laughed. "How can a handful of men manage three thousand prisoners without strict discipline?" he said.

He had a point. Many prisoners complained about their punishments. But I knew I had done wrong and was ready to face the consequences. I paid for my mistakes. I took my punishment like a man.

The prison governor was a strict disciplinarian, yet I sensed a streak of kindness in him. In a role like his, toughness was necessary; otherwise, the prisoners would overrun you. He bore the physical scars of assaults from inmates as proof. Prison, after all, is a place of punishment for those who have broken the law, and the only ways out are through the main gate as a free man or in a coffin. Many inmates didn't see it that way.

Prison could also be a place to meet interesting people, especially in the exercise yard, depending on who you hung out with. I met a man, a university professor serving ten years for passing information about atomic bomb development to the Soviets. He said he wasn't a traitor, that he was doing what was right.

"If only one country holds the secrets to the atomic bomb, it could become greedy and oppressive," he argued. "But if the secrets are shared among many nations, the threat of war decreases as they fear one another."

I nodded. He was right.

My sentence ended. Two British officials from the Home Office came to the prison. They took me from my cell. I thought about what waited for me in Spain. Franco ruled there and had sided with the Germans. I had served with the Free French instead of the Spanish army. That was my duty. But Franco's officials wouldn't see it that way. I would go to prison again. Maybe for years. The officials put me in a car. "We're taking you to a ship bound for Spain," one said. "But first, you can see your children. One visit. To say goodbye."

I knew I would never see them again.

10

FAREWELL TO INNOCENCE

The farewell was hard. My children clung to me as they cried. I couldn't help but think about the cruelty of it. They were separating a man from his family. I didn't blame the authorities. They had warned me but I had thought they were joking. It was no joke.

Tears came to my eyes. Thick tears. They led me away. I knew I would never see my children again as they escorted me to the ship. It was bound for South America via Vigo in Spain. British Home Office officials handed me over to the ship's captain. They gave him strict instructions to put me ashore in Vigo and the captain locked me in the ship's brig. It was a cabin they had converted into a prison cell, barred doors and windows.

Before we reached Spain, the ship stopped at Cherbourg-en-Cotentin, a port city in Normandy, France. French security police boarded. They were there as a courtesy. As they passed my cell, I recognized the commanding officer. I don't know why I called out to him. This was the same commanding officer I had once threatened to shoot at a Free French camp in England. That night, he had been drunk and refused to give me the password to re-enter the camp late.

The officer approached my cell. For a few minutes, he looked at me. Then recognition came to his face. "What are you doing here?" he asked.

I explained everything that had happened since I left the Free French. I told him about my impending forced return to Spain. The officer listened without interrupting.

"Do you want to go to Spain?" he asked when I finished.

I told him no.

"Well," he said, "the only way they'll take you to Spain is over my dead body".

The captain spoke up. "But this is my ship," he said.

The French officer replied sharply. "And this is my water. Don't forget that. You are in French territory."

"The trouble with you British," the officer continued, "is that you only remember the bad things a man has done. What about the good things? He served under my command in the Free French. Sending him back to Spain now is like delivering him to the firing squad."

Their voices rose as the argument grew heated. Others gathered around. Finally, the British captain left. He sent a message to England. I waited in my cell while the French officer stayed on deck. Hours passed.

I didn't know what had happened in their discussions. But two hours later, I was standing free on French soil. I sought out the French officer and apologized for my behaviour at the camp in England. I explained I had to obey my orders.

He laughed. "That was a long time ago," he said and called the other officers over.

I nodded and said, "I could have shot you".

He called the other officers over and told them how he came to know me. Some came to greet me. Others began arranging French identification papers for me and collected some money to help me on my way.

"Now you are a free man," their commanding officer told me. "You can go to any part of France you wish. If I were you, I'd go to Rouen. From there, you can ship out to any part of the world you want".

He knew I had to keep moving.

I thanked them and that afternoon I took a train to Rouen. The city was a port and the war had bombed it hard. Many buildings stood broken, their walls cracked and windows gone. Rubble lined some streets. But the cafes were open. People walked the streets and ships moved in the harbour. Normandy's capital city was coming back.

After a week in Rouen, I signed onto a Norwegian ship that was filled with rich passengers. I was recruited as an able seaman. We set sail from France with our first port, Liverpool. I stayed on board there. But the images of my children crying haunted me. I had thought I would never see them again. I couldn't stand it so just before the ship was due to depart, I jumped ship and caught a train to London.

I arrived at midnight and went straight to my home. My mother in-law answered the door and gasped.

"The children", I said.

"Asleep," she said.

"Where is she?" I asked.

"Out," she said. "But it's odd she left the children."

When Dorothy returned, I asked her where she had been.

"Out with my boyfriend," she said.

It felt like a knife as I stood there. But I had done the same to her. I knew that and I said nothing.

The next day, I found the boyfriend and confronted him.

"Well, now what are you going to do about it?" he said.

I wanted to hit him. But I didn't. "I'm going to fight for custody of my children," I said.

I went to the police to report my Dorothy's affair and tell them I wanted to gain custody of my children. They asked for my papers. I had none. I was in the country illegally, so they called Scotland Yard. Two detectives came and took me away. I found myself in another prison. I never saw my children. Two months later, they shipped me back to France.

In Le Havre, I signed onto another Norwegian ship. The crew looked like professional tramps. We set sail for Casablanca with the chief mate on the same watch as me. He was a constant drunk. One night, he stumbled onto the bridge, ordering me to change course every five minutes. The ship zigzagged wildly and we nearly collided with an oncoming vessel.

I refused his commands.

We fought right there on the bridge. The captain and other crew members arrived and saw the state of the chief mate. The captain stripped him of his duties immediately.

We docked in Casablanca. As usual, I went ashore alone. I wandered until I heard music. It came from a place called Café Le France. It was a dance hall. I had been feeling low. Depressed. Melancholic. But I didn't think wallowing would help anyone. When I heard the tango, I couldn't resist and went inside. The orchestra was playing Gerardo Matos Rodriguez's La Cumparsita. My favourite. I felt the urge to dance. In Casablanca, they speak both French and Spanish. I asked a girl in French if she wanted to dance. She declined. I tried again in Spanish with another girl. She declined too.

Undeterred, I muttered to myself, "Tonight, I'm dancing, come what may".

Then I saw a tall girl standing alone. I asked her if she would like to dance, and to my surprise, she agreed. We danced. We chatted in English. When the dance ended, I walked her home.

Along the way, she asked about my nationality. Being Spanish or French might not sit well here. The war was over, but the shadows remained. Colonial tensions lingered.

"I'm American," I said.

She wrapped her arms around me. "We love Americans back home," she said.

We walked in silence for a moment.

"My family is Jewish," she said.

"So am I," I said.

She smiled and took my hand. "Come," she said. "Meet my family".

She took me to her home that night to meet everyone. Two brothers. Two sisters. Her mother. They were Spanish Jews who owned several jewellery shops across North Africa. While her family chatted away in Spanish, she kindly translated their words into English for me. After all, I was supposed to be an American. The next day, she had business away from Casablanca, so she took me with her. For a week, while the ship was docked, we were inseparable. It was better than being alone.

Ten days later, as we were preparing to leave, one of the ship's engines failed. The captain summoned me and explained, "We can't head to France because of the engine. We're off to Norway, and from there, you'll go to Spain."

"I signed on in France", I protested. "You need to send me back there."

He refused, citing the cost. We argued. Finally, as the ship began to move, I climbed onto the rail and jumped off. I swam to the dock and waved at the captain yelling, red-faced from the deck.

It was late, around ten-thirty at night. I had only a few francs—just enough for the taxi fare. I directed the driver to the girl's place. When she opened the door she stared at me. II was dripping wet from the swim in the harbour.

"What are you doing here?" she said.

"I jumped ship," I said. "Had a fight with the captain."

She looked at me for a long moment. Then she stepped back and opened the door wider.

"Come in," she said. "You're soaking wet."

She found me a spare room. Her brothers lent me clothes, since all of mine had sailed away with the ship. A suit, shirts, underwear. They were generous but she kept hinting about marriage. I couldn't do that. I was a deserter and needed to leave Casablanca. I spent days at the waterfront, trying to find a ship. Three weeks passed and nothing.

One evening, she came to me with news. "I have a surprise for you," she said.

"What is it?" I asked.

"I spoke to someone at the American Consulate," she said. "They want to meet you tomorrow".

My stomach tightened.

"That's good," I said.

The next day, we headed to the consulate. On the way, I said, "You should go in first. Have them check my papers. If you still want to talk after, we can".

She nodded and went inside. I stood on the street. Then I walked to the waterfront and the Swedish ship was still there—the one I'd tried before. This time they were hiring. It was spotless and had an international crew.

I never saw her again.

The ship was bound for France at midnight. I couldn't go ashore, so I stayed onboard with the clothes I had. Some of the crew pitched in to help. The cook and the steward were women. One of them was engaged to the Chief Mate. She had dark hair and stood straight when she walked. We set sail for France and then received orders for Casablanca.

In Casablanca, I went ashore and line up at the bus ticket office. A young boy asked me for help getting his ticket. We struck up a friendship, and he later introduced me to his family, Spanish Jews—kind folks with seven siblings and another on the way.

The boy was seventeen and worked as a mechanic. He drove me around the city in his car and as we passed the docks he stopped the car. He looked out at the ships for a long time.

"You work on a ship," he said.

"Yes."

"I want to work on a ship too."

"You're a mechanic," I said.

"I can learn," he said. "I watch the ships every day."

"I'll see what I can do," I promised.

We grew close over those days in port. One morning the Chief Mate sent for me. "Richards is in hospital," he said. "Fever. They're keeping him."

"How long?"

"Two weeks. Maybe more." He looked at me. "We sail in three days."

I thought of the boy. "I know someone here," I said. "He wants to go to sea."

The Chief Mate nodded. "Bring him tomorrow. We'll look him over. "

The boy joined the ship as a wiper, cleaning and helping in the engine room. Since he spoke no English, he was placed in my watch. His family was happy.

Our return to France brought heavy weather. The boy was sick from the roll of the ship. He lay in his bunk, unable to stand. As the ship rolled, he held tightly to the rail of the bunk. I went to see him in the morning and at night.

"Pull yourself together, or you'll die," I warned him in Spanish.

He listened. After two days he got up and learned to move with the ship. I showed him how to do the work, and he did it.

We reached France and loaded cargo. Then we received orders to return to Casablanca.

When we docked, I went alone to see the boy's family. The house was quiet. Black cloth hung over the door. Inside the children sat against the wall. The oldest girl held the baby. The baby was small and red and made no sound.

"Your mother," I said to the oldest girl.

She nodded.

I stood there. I didn't really know them well, but my eyes stung and I did not wipe them. The girl looked at me and then looked down at the baby.

I walked back to the ship slowly. The boy was on deck coiling rope. I watched him work for a while, then I called him over.

"You must go ashore," I said.

"Why?"

I looked at him. "Your mother is dead."

He stared at me while his hands still held the rope, his face empty. Then he dropped the rope and walked to the rail. He looked down at the dock for a long time then he went down the gangway without looking back.

He came back after dark. His shirt was torn and there was blood on his hands. The Chief Mate was waiting for me on deck.

"Where is he?"

"He came back."

"Keep him in your watch tonight."

I went to find the boy. He was in his bunk facing the wall. I sat on the bunk across from him but he did not turn around. I stayed there for a while and then I left.

In the morning his bunk was empty. I went on deck and asked the crew, but no one had seen him. I went ashore and walked to the house. There was no one there so I walked through the market asking for him and then to the harbour asking at every ship. No one had seen him.

I dragged myself back to the ship and found that we had received orders for Santa Cruz de Tenerife in the Canary Islands. There was another Spaniard onboard, another refugee from the Civil War. I found him on deck.

"We're going to Tenerife," I said.

He looked at the water and said nothing.

"We have no choice. It's too late to turn back."

He nodded and went below. When we sighted Tenerife he did not come up. We entered the harbor with naval vessels all around us and Spanish Nationalist flags on the buildings. The police came aboard at the dock and an officer walked up to me.

"Spaniards onboard?"

"Two," I said. "My mate and me."

"Your politics?"

"We only talk about women," I said.

The officer laughed and waved us through.

Some of us went ashore. The other Spaniard stayed on the ship, and we walked into town like tourists though there were few of them about. At a café we met a singer from Madrid. He was black and smartly dressed. Everyone called him "Nacho" and he seemed popular. Two girls worked for him, one had red hair, and one was blonde and they sat at our table.

"You are English?" the singer asked.

"Australian," I said.

We spoke in English. The girls spoke English too. They asked about Australia, and we told them stories about something we knew nothing. Nacho bought drinks and the girls laughed at our stories. one touching my arm when she laughed.

"You will come tonight to hear me sing?" Nacho asked.

"Yes," I said.

We listened to him that night. He was good, really good. The girls sat with us as we drank and watched him crooning away. The blonde girl sat close and when Nacho finished, she asked if we would walk with them.

We walked through the streets the girls speaking to each other in Spanish. One of them looked at me and said something to the other girl. They both laughed. I kept walking. When they asked us questions in English we answered. Then they went back to Spanish, talking fast and looking at us.

We walked back near dawn. The ship's whistle blew and we were late.

'We have to go,' I said to the girls in Spanish.

They suddenly stopped walking. The blonde girl stared at me. The other one's mouth opened.

'You speak Spanish,' the blonde said.

'Yes.'

'All night?'

'Yes.'

Her face went red, and she turned to her friend. They looked at each other and turned and walked away fast without saying goodbye. As we watched them go and my mate started to laugh. I laughed too. We ran for the ship.

11

THE CAPTAIN'S WIFE

We sailed from Tenerife to Marseille. I went ashore the first night and found a club. It was dark and loud with music. I sat at the bar and looked around. A woman sat alone at a table near the back. She had dark hair, wore a green dress and was drinking alone.

I walked over and said: "Mind if I sit?"

"Please," she said.

I sat down and the waiter brought drinks.

"What's a woman like you doing here alone?" I asked.

She laughed. "Waiting for my husband. He's a sea captain."

"Should I be worried?"

"Don't worry," she said. "He won't bite."

We talked and she asked about the ship. I told her about Casablanca and the storms. She listened and smiled. We ordered more drinks.

"You want to dance?" I asked.

"Yes."

We danced. The club was full. People from everywhere. French and Spanish and Greeks. The music was loud.

When we came back to the table a man was standing there. He wore a captain's uniform. My captain. He looked at me and then at his wife.

"This is one of yours," she said to him.

He nodded and sat down and ordered a drink. He didn't look at me again. He drank and watched the room. His wife looked at me and smiled.

"We can dance more," she said.

I looked at the captain. He was watching the band and seemed not to care.

"All right," I said.

We danced the rest of the night. The captain sat at the table and drank, never looking our way. When the music stopped, we went back to the table.

"Time to go," the captain said to his wife.

"Good night then," she said to him.

He left and we stayed.

He didn't love his wife. She was wealthy though, a major shareholder in the company we worked for, and her word was law. While the captain drank, she made plans. The club closed and she asked me to escort her to her hotel in Marseille. That night we became lovers. From France we travelled to Germany and then to Denmark and through her influence we secured a contract along the Swedish coast. The captain's wife wasn't stunning. She was no Venus, but she was attractive enough and I grew fond of her.

In a town called Marmol my shipmate and I went to the movies while she was away. Afterward, we met two lovely women. "Are you seamen?" they asked. "Do you have any drinks on board?" We said we did hoping to impress them. Back on the ship all we had was orange juice so I went into the engine room and grabbed a bottle of alcohol and mixed it with the juice, sugar, and coffee. My friend poured the drinks and the women laughed at how bad it tasted. The blonde one left. The other stayed and talked with me while my friend went on deck. Later she came to my cabin. They came back the next day at two in the morning and brought vodka. I didn't drink so I sat with them and we talked until dawn. We had a grand time in Marmol and we stayed three more days until the ship was ready to leave.

Three months later we were ordered back to London. I couldn't betray the captain. He had been decent to me so I went to his cabin and told him everything. I told him about the deportation from England and about my family and the situation I was in. He listened and didn't say anything for a while. Then he said he would help. When we docked in London my mother-in-law was waiting on the wharf and my children were with her. I couldn't believe it. They came aboard and stayed with me until the ship departed for Sweden. I wasn't allowed ashore, so the captain arranged for my children to visit me on the ship. This brought me great happiness. We kept running between London and Sweden and each time we docked the children came to see me. The captain never said anything about his wife, and I never understood why he seemed so content, knowing what he knew.

After three months we returned to London, and Dorothy came to visit for the first time. She was crying when she came aboard.

"What's wrong?" I asked.

"My boyfriend left me," she said.

I looked at her. "You'll find someone else."

"I'm going to have a baby."

I wasn't angry anymore and I'd lost my feelings for her, but I felt sorry for her standing there. "You came back to me?" I asked.

"Yes."

"I'll take your child and give my name as if it was mine,"
I said. "But you have to go to the Home Office and ask them
to let me stay in England."

"Yes, I will," she said. "And I'll be good to you."

We kissed for the first time since separating and it felt
good to hold her again. I returned to Sweden and bought
baby clothes in every port and spent a small fortune on an
expensive coat for a child that wasn't mine.

Back in London nobody was waiting for me, so I phoned
Dorothy from the ship.

"I'm back with my boyfriend again," she said.

I didn't say anything. I put down the phone and walked
out on deck. The water was dark. I went to the captain's
cabin.

"If you don't do something, I think I'll jump ship," I said.

The captain nodded and reached for the telephone.
Within the hour, two officials came aboard. They put me on
another vessel and sent me to Las Palmas where I stayed at
the British sailors' home near the port. It was run by British
priest who couldn't speak Spanish. During an argument with
one of the servants, he turned to me.

"Do you speak Spanish?" he said.

"Yes."

"I need you," he went on.

He asked me to stay and run the place. I spoke to the
servants in Spanish did the shopping and handled the bills.
The British Consul came by after a week and looked over the
books. He nodded and said he would pay me. I lived well. My
room was on the ground floor and I left the window
unlocked so I could slip in at night without the priest
knowing.

This sailors' home was on one end of the town, at a place
called Puerto La Luz, about twenty minutes' drive to the city
centre. One day, I found myself out of money and I was at

the taxi stand trying to sell a beautiful belt I had from India to a taxi driver. Just then, an American sailor approached, asking the driver to take him into town. The driver didn't understand, so I translated for the sailor.

The American looked at me. "You speak Spanish?"

"Yes."

"Forget the belt and come with us," he said. "I'll pay your fare."

We drove into the heart of the city to a street lined with nightclubs and houses of pleasure. This was Franco's Spain and few foreigners, especially English speakers, came. The regime kept the country closed and most people had never learned English. The American knew where he was going and took me to Casa Pepe, a place away from the tourist hotels where the locals went. The women working there were Spanish and spoke no English. Foreign sailors came to the port, but communication was difficult. The American bought me a drink and asked me to translate for him. I did and he paid me for my help.

Word spread among the taxi drivers that I could translate. The next day three drivers came to the sailors' home looking for me. They needed someone who could speak English and Spanish to help with the passengers from the ships. Every day passenger ships docked at Muelle del Generalísimo Franco and the drivers needed to know where the passengers wanted to go. They made me their agent. My job was simple. I stood on the gangway and directed the drivers to the passengers' destinations. Each driver tossed me five pesetas. I lived comfortably and never worried about my next meal. By day, I was the model Christian from the mission. By night I prowled the streets and slipped back through my window in the early morning hours.

One afternoon, as I sat at a waterfront bar, a bloody fight broke out between foreign seamen and Spanish sailors. The police soon rushed in. One officer was trying to question a Norwegian sailor, but they couldn't understand each other. I walked over.

"I can translate," I said.

The officer looked at me. "You speak Norwegian?"

"Yes. A little. I worked on Norwegian ships."

He ended up taking me to the police station where about ten foreign seamen were detained and none of the officers could communicate with them. And so it went. I translated for two hours and when I finished a man in plain clothes came up to me. He was the chief of police.

"What's your name?" he asked.

I told him.

"If you're ever in trouble here in Las Palmas, come to me," he said.

My language skills opened doors I never expected. I had money and connections and a room at the sailors' home. I lived well for a time.

One afternoon I met a girl at the cinema. She was well-dressed and her family seemed well-off. I kept my mornings at the sailors' home looking respectable but at night I went out with her. We spent weeks like this, but the pull of my children was always there.

A letter came from my mother-in-law arrived one day. One of the children was sick and I had to return to England.

I went to the office of Miller Shipping Company on the waterfront, agents who handled all the maritime affairs in Las Palmas and managed both foreign and British vessels coming through the port. The manager was also the British Honorary Consul, and I had worked with him before through my job directing passengers at the docks. He knew me as a reliable worker.

"I need to ship out again," I told him. "My child is sick in England."

He looked through his files. "You're registered as a seaman. No issues I can see here." He was more of a businessman than a diplomat. His files contained shipping records and crew manifests, not deportation orders from London. Those records, if they existed anywhere in Las Palmas, were buried in some official file he never saw. A few days later he sent word that there was a Dutch ship needing a fireman. It was bound for Holland and from there I could make my way to England. I knew the work would be gruelling, but I signed on anyway. It would be a week's journey.

I left Las Palmas not knowing if I would return. The girl came to see me off at the dock, but we didn't say much. The work as fireman was hard. I shovelled coal into the boilers for four-hour watches and the heat was brutal. There was an old Dutch fireman who worked with me, and he moved slowly. I did most of the work. After each watch I collapsed in my bunk.

The weather stayed warm. After three days I asked the chief fireman where in Holland we were headed.

He looked at me. "Holland?"

"Yes. Which port?"

He laughed. "We're not going to Holland. Not yet."

"Where are we going?"

"West Africa first," he said. "Then East Africa. Then Holland."

"Miller said this was a week to Holland."

The chief fireman shrugged. "Miller says what he needs to say to get crew."

I had been deceived. The voyage would be months, not days. My child was sick, and I was sailing away from England, not toward it. There was nothing I could do. I was signed on, and the ship was at sea, so I went back to the engine room and shoveled more coal.

12

ROWING TO DOVER

y cabin mate was a young Dutchman who hadn't spoken to me the entire voyage. One day I asked him why.

"You're Spanish," he said.

"So?"

"You worked in Spain. You speak Spanish. Same thing."

"I was just working there."

"My uncle fought Franco. He died at the Ebro."

He looked at me with contempt. "And you're a fireman. You shovel coal."

That was all. He went back to his bunk and we never spoke again. The work in the engine room continued. Weeks passed until we finally docked in East Africa to take on cargo.

The port was Mombasa, and the place was hot and smelled of spices and diesel fuel. The chief fireman said we had three days while they loaded. I went ashore the first day looking for a post office near the harbor and bought paper and an envelope. I wrote to my mother-in-law and told her I was on a Dutch ship heading to Amsterdam and would try to reach England from there. I gave her the address of Miller Shipping Company in Rotterdam and asked her to write there. I kept walking through the area when a boy came up to me at the dock gate. He was about twelve and wore shorts and a white shirt.

"You need guide?" he asked in English.

"How much?"

"One shilling."

I gave him it to him from the coins just given to me and he led me away from the docks. We walked through narrow streets with shabby concrete buildings that had shops on the ground floor. The heat was worse away from the water. After twenty minutes we came to an open market with stalls under canvas and cloth awnings.

"My family," he said. He pointed to a stall selling fruit and vegetables.

His mother was there with two younger children. She looked at me and said something in Swahili to the boy. He answered and she smiled and cut up a mango for me. It was sweet and I ate it standing there in the shade of the awning. They didn't speak much English, but the boy translated. I learned his name was Joseph. His father worked on the railway, and they had the stall four days a week. I came back the next day and the day after that. They fed me both times and on the third day Joseph's mother gave me a cloth bundle with fruit wrapped inside for the voyage. I stood at the market thinking about staying. I could disappear into the city. Find work. Send money to my children somehow. But I had no papers for Kenya and no way to get back to England except by ship.

The ship's whistle sounded from the harbor. One long blast. We were departing. Joseph walked me back to the docks. At the gate his mother had sent small carved animals wrapped in paper. Gifts for my children.

"Come back," Joseph said.

I shook his hand and went up the gangway. The ship pulled away from the dock, and I stood on deck watching the port disappear. I thought about the Dutch crew who wouldn't speak to me and about Joseph's family who had fed me without asking anything in return.

The voyage back took three months.

The chief fireman died two weeks out of Mombasa. His heart gave out in the engine room, and they buried him at sea. I did all the work after that. Four-hour watches shovelling coal with no one to spell me. My hands split open and wouldn't heal. The salt from my sweat got into the cracks and burned. I wrapped them in rags, but the rags stuck to the wounds. After each watch I peeled them off and the bleeding started again. The heat in the engine room got worse as we crossed the equator. I drank water constantly but stayed thirsty. My clothes were always soaked. At night I dreamed about cool places. We finally stopped in Lagos for two days to take on coal. I stayed on the ship. In Dakar we stopped again. More coal. The Dutch crew went ashore but I had no money left.

In the Atlantic the chief mate told me we would reach Amsterdam in two weeks. The weather turned cold, and I had no warm clothes. In the engine room I was still hot but going on deck the wind cut through my shirt. We reached Amsterdam on a grey morning. I had lost weight, and my hands were covered in scars. Three months had felt like a year.

The captain asked if I would sign on again.

"Even if you paid me in gold, I wouldn't stay another minute," I said.

I went ashore with my wages. The shipping company's agent met me at the dock giving me an address in Rotterdam.

"Report there tomorrow," he said. "Everything is arranged for your passage to England."

That night I walked through Amsterdam. I found a bar and drank beer and slept in a cheap hotel near the station. The next morning I took the train to Rotterdam. The shipping office was in a building near the port and I gave my name to the clerk.

"I'm here about my passage to England," I said.

He looked through his files. "Your papers aren't ready. Come back tomorrow."

I came back the next day. The same clerk was there.

"Still not ready. Come back Monday."

On Monday I went back. A different clerk told me to wait. I waited three hours. He told me to come back on Wednesday.

On Wednesday I went to the immigration office instead.

"I need papers to get to England," I told the officer. "The shipping company can't help me."

He looked at my papers. "Wait here."

Two officers came and took me to a detention facility where they put me in a cell. I asked when I would be released, and they said it depended on my paperwork. The cell was small, and I was alone. I had nothing to read and no one to talk to. Days passed. I counted them by the meals they brought. After two weeks a letter arrived from England through the Rotterdam office of the shipping company. My child was still sick and after another two weeks they released me from detention. An officer gave me back my papers and told me I had to leave the Netherlands within forty-eight hours. I had enough money left from my ship's wages for a train ticket and took the first train to Calais. From there I would try to get across the Channel to England somehow.

In Calais I went to the ferry terminal. I bought a ticket to Dover and had a little left to keep the hunger away for a few days. The ferry crossed at night. When we docked at Dover I joined the line for immigration control. The officer looked at my papers and checked something in a ledger. Then he looked up at me.

"You've been here before," he said.

"Yes. My family is in England."

He stamped nothing. "Step aside please."

Two other officers took me to a room asking questions. How did I leave England? Why was I trying to return? Where had I been? I told them about my sick child and showed them my mother-in-law's letter. They read it and put it aside.

"You were deported," one officer said. "You're prohibited from re-entering the United Kingdom."

"My child is sick."

"That doesn't change your status."

They held me overnight and put me on the ferry back to Calais the next morning. I stood on deck as we crossed. The water was calm. I watched small fishing boats working between the ferry lanes. Some were close to the French coast and others worked near the English side. Twenty-one miles between the two shores. The crossing took ninety minutes by ferry, and I thought about how long it would take in a small boat. Three hours maybe. Four in bad weather. The fishing boats made the crossing look easy.

When we docked at Calais, I walked off the ferry with the other passengers. I had no money left and nowhere to go. But I knew the fishing boats worked these waters every day. Twenty-one miles wasn't a great distance for them. The day was clear and as I walked to the harbour I could see across the Channel. The White Cliffs of Dover stood out against the blue sky. England was right there. My child was somewhere beyond those cliffs.

I spent the afternoon walking the docks looking for fishing boats and came across an older man working on his nets. I showed him my watch. It was a good watch from my smuggling days. I'd kept it all these years.

"I need to get to Dover," I said. "I'll give you this watch."

He looked at the watch, then handed it back. "Not enough. And too much trouble with the police."

By evening I sat on the beach. There was a small rowboat pulled up on the sand. I looked at it for a long time. The lights of Dover were visible across the water. I waited until dark and pushed the boat into the water and started rowing toward England. The sea was calm at first. After an hour my hands were bleeding. The oars were rough wood and had worn through the skin. I kept rowing but the lights of Dover stayed in the same place on the horizon. After two hours I realized the tide was pulling me sideways. I was rowing hard but moving parallel to the coast, not across. My arms burned and my back cramped but I kept pulling the oars.

A bright light swept across the water and fixed on me. I shielded my eyes. The engine of a boat grew louder as two officers in a French Coast Guard vessel came alongside.

"What are you doing?" one shouted down.

"Going to England."

"In that?" He looked at the small rowboat, then at me. "You won't make it. The tide will push you to Belgium before you get halfway."

They pulled me aboard and towed the rowboat back to Calais. At the harbor they turned me over to the police who held me overnight and released me in the morning with a warning to stay away from the harbour. I went back to the harbour anyway and watched the trucks loading onto the Dover ferry. The drivers parked their trucks on the car deck and went upstairs to the passenger areas while the trucks sat empty during the crossing.

I watched the loading pattern for two days. Ferry workers checked vehicles at the entrance ramp. Drivers showed tickets and police walked the car deck before departure. I needed to get on after the workers checked but before the police did their final sweep.

On the third evening I waited by the terminal fence. The ferry was loading. I watched until most of the trucks were aboard. The ticket attendant turned away to help a driver with papers so I walked quickly past the booth and down the ramp to the car deck.

A ferry worker shouted at me. I kept walking toward the trucks and he kept shouting. I found a canvas-sided truck near the back and climbed in. I pulled the tarpaulin over me and lay flat behind the cargo crates. I heard footsteps on the metal deck. The ferry worker was looking for me. The footsteps came closer and stopped near my truck. I didn't move. After a minute the footsteps went away.

The ferry engines started, and we began crossing the Channel. After ninety minutes the engines changed pitch as we were docking at Dover. I heard the driver get back in the truck and start the engine. We drove off the ferry. When the truck stopped, I heard voices—the immigration checkpoint. The driver said something as papers rustled. Then we drove on. Ten minutes later the truck stopped again - at a traffic light. I pushed aside the tarpaulin, jumped out, and ran off fast. I was in Dover.

I had French and Dutch money but no English pounds. I couldn't exchange it at a bank without identification.

I walked along the main road toward London. Canterbury was fifteen miles from Dover. I reached it by late afternoon and found a roadside cafe near the edge of town. Lorries were parked outside.

I went in and sat at the counter near a driver who was eating eggs and chips. I waited until he finished.

"Excuse me," I said. "Would you exchange some foreign currency for English pounds?"

He looked at me. "How much?"

I showed him the Dutch guilders and French francs. He counted it.

"I'll give you three pounds for this," he said.

It wasn't a fair rate, but I needed English money. I took it and he bought me breakfast and said he was driving to London. I could ride with him if I wanted.

We reached London that evening, dropping me off at Whitechapel. I walked to the address where my wife had been living. It was a boarding house near Commercial Road.

I knocked on the door. My mother-in-law answered looking surprised.

"You got my letter," she said.

"Yes."

"I didn't think you'd... I mean, how did you get here?"

"I need to see the children."

She looked over her shoulder into the flat, then back at me. "You can't stay. If they find you here—"

"I know."

She let me in and led me to the children in the back room.

They were older than I remembered. My daughter didn't recognize me at first.

My wife came home an hour later. She wasn't alone. There was a man with her. When she saw me she stopped in the doorway.

"This is where you've been living?" I said.

"You were deported," she said. "You weren't coming back."

"I'm here now."

The man she was with looked uncomfortable and he left without saying anything.

I stayed that night. The next day I looked for work. Without proper papers I couldn't get legal employment, so I found a dishwashing job at a club in Soho using a false name. The owner didn't ask questions and he paid cash weekly.

For two weeks I worked at the club and stayed at the boarding house. My wife's boyfriend came around during the day when I was at work. My mother-in-law told me about it. One night my wife said she needed money for the rent. I gave her what I had from my earnings at the club. The next week she asked for more. When I said I didn't have it, she said she would go to the police and tell them I was in the country illegally.

"You'll go to prison," she said.

"So will you for helping me," I said.

"They won't care about that. They want you."

The blackmail went on for three weeks. Every time I had wages from the club, my wife asked for more money. When I didn't have enough, she threatened to call the police. One afternoon I came back to the boarding house early. My wife's boyfriend was there, he was sitting at the kitchen table drinking tea.

"We need to talk," he said.

My mother-in-law took the children to another room.

"I was with her while you were in prison," he said.

"I figure as much."

"The girl might be mine."

I didn't say anything.

"She doesn't know for certain," he said. "The timing was close."

"She's my daughter," I said.

"Maybe."

I left the flat and walked. I didn't know where I was going. I ended up near Whitehall. The Home Office building stood at the end of the street. I thought about turning myself in. If I did, they would deport me and I would never see the children again. But if I stayed, I would be caught eventually.

My wife would make sure of it. I walked to the building. There were guards at the entrance and I went to the reception desk.

"I need to speak to someone about immigration," I said.

The clerk looked at me. "Do you have an appointment?"

"No."

"You'll need to go to the Immigration Office in Croydon for that."

"But I'm here now," I said.

He picked up a telephone and spoke to someone. After a few minutes a man in a suit came down the stairs.

"You wanted to speak about immigration?" he said.

"Yes."

"Come with me."

He took me to an office on the first floor. I sat down and told him I had entered the country illegally. I told him about my wife and children. I told him I wanted to give myself up. He listened without interrupting and when I finished, he picked up the telephone.

"Wait here," he said.

Twenty minutes later two police officers came to the office. They asked me to stand then one of them put handcuffs on me.

"You're being detained under the Immigration Act," he said.

They took me out through a back entrance, put me in a police van and drove to Brixton Prison.

They held me in prison for two weeks while the immigration officials processed the deportation order. An officer came to interview me about how I had entered the country. I told him about the truck on the ferry while he took notes.

"You were caught off Calais trying to row across the Channel," he said, reading from a file.

"Yes."

"Then you stowed away on a ferry."

"Yes."

He closed the file. "You'll be deported to France. You're banned from re-entering the United Kingdom for five years."

"What about my children?"

"That's not my concern," he replied.

Two weeks later, two officers escorted me to Southampton via train from London. At Southampton docks we boarded a ferry to Le Havre. The officers stayed with me during the crossing and when we reached Le Havre they handed me over to French immigration officials on the dock. The officers returned to England on the same ferry. I had no money and nowhere to go. In Le Havre I would have to start again.

13

NIGHT IN THE CASBAH

In Le Havre I looked for work on ships. After three days I found a Swedish freighter heading to Casablanca. They needed a deckhand, and I signed on. We left the next morning. In the Bay of Biscay we hit a storm with waves were thirty feet high. The captain changed course to ride it out. We heard on the radio that another cargo ship had gone down in the same storm, which lasted two days. When it cleared, we continued south to Casablanca.

At the port I was paid off and had enough money for a few weeks. I walked through the port district looking for another ship. When I asked around about ships hiring crew someone told me the chief mate on an Estonian ship docked nearby was Spanish. I went to find him. The ship was at the far end of the dock where I found the chief mate on deck checking cargo. I called out to him in Spanish.

"I heard you're from Spain," I said.

"Barcelona," he said. "You?"

"Madrid."

"Good to meet someone from home. What brings you here?"

"Looking for work."

"We're full up. But I'm here for three days. Let me buy you dinner tonight. We can go to the Casbah."

"I know the Casbah," I said. "It's not safe."

"Yeh, I've heard stories. Sounds interesting."

"The police don't go inside," I added.

"Even better," he said.

I didn't want to go but he was a fellow Spaniard so that night we took a taxi to the Casbah gates.

Inside, the streets were narrow and dark. Music came from the buildings – Arab music with drums and strings. Five women approached us on the street. They were Arab prostitutes.

One of them touched the chief mate's arm. "Come to my house," she said in French.

"No thank you," I said.

"Yes," the chief mate jumped in. "Let's go."

We followed them to a building at the end of the street. Inside there was a small room with cushions on the floor and a table. The women undressed and started dancing. The chief mate laughed and ordered drinks. They brought bottles of cheap French wine and a long wooden pipe. The chief mate drank and smoked. The women sat with us and kept filling his glass and refilling the pipe with kif. I didn't drink or smoke. The hours passed slowly. I had sat in rooms like this in Marseille and Amsterdam and Tangier. Different women, different ports. The music and the smoke and the waiting were always the same. Here I just watched the door.

At three in the morning I checked my watch. The chief mate's eyes were half-closed. I wanted to leave.

"We should go," I said.

"Not yet," he said. "One more drink."

One of the women brought the bill and set it on the table. The chief mate picked it up and looked at it. Then he looked at me.

"I don't have any money," he said.

I stared at him. "What?"

"I thought you would pay."

"You invited me."

"I don't have anything," he said.

The women were watching us. One of them went to the door and stood in front of it. In the Casbah, if you couldn't pay, they would beat or even kill you. The police never came inside.

"I need to use the bathroom," I said.

I went through a curtain at the back. The bathroom was small and dirty. Behind the door in the next room hung a man's gown. I checked the pockets. There was a wallet stuffed with bills. I counted them quickly. Several thousand francs.

I went back to the main room and one of the women was talking to the chief mate in Arabic. I couldn't understand what she was saying but her voice was angry.

"How much do we owe?" I asked in French.

"Twenty thousand francs," she said.

I took out the money and counted out twenty-five thousand francs. I put the bills on the table.

"Let's go," I said to the chief mate.

He was looking at the money. "Where did you get that?"

"Let's go now!"

He stood up slowly. The woman at the door moved aside. We walked out into the street.

In the taxi back to the port I told him what I had done. He didn't say anything. At the docks he got out and walked to his ship. I never saw him again. I walked back through the port district. The streets were empty, and dawn was breaking over the harbour. I thought about the Casbah and the women and the wallet behind the door and how lucky I had been back there. I had been coming to ports like this for ten years. Casablanca, Marseille, Amsterdam, Liverpool. The ports were different, but the nights were all the same. Men drinking and smoking and paying women. Ships leaving at dawn.

I was tired.

I slept for a few hours in my room. It was small and cheap, with a narrow bed and a washbasin. The window looked out on an alley. When I woke it was afternoon. I went back to the docks to look for work. There was a Norwegian freighter loading cargo for Marseille. The captain needed a deckhand so I signed on. We would sail in two days. The next morning a dock worker I knew found me on the ship.

"Don't go ashore," he said.

"Why not?"

"Men from the Casbah are looking for you. They're asking about a foreigner who was at the club two nights ago."

I stayed on the ship and worked for three days below deck while the cargo was loaded. I watched the dock from the porthole. On the third day we sailed. The ship was good. It was clean and well-maintained. The cabins had proper bunks, and the galley served hot meals three times a day. After the cheap room in Casablanca, it felt comfortable.

The crew was mixed. There were Norwegians, Finns, Germans, a Dane, and two Greeks. We worked well together. The captain ran a tight ship, but he was fair. We made good time to Marseille. The weather held and the sea was calm. In Marseille the captain called us together.

"We have a new contract," he said. "Back to North Africa. Casablanca and Tangier. Anyone who doesn't want to go can leave the ship here."

I didn't leave. I needed the work.

The pay was good. Better than most ships. At first I didn't understand why. Then on the second voyage I learned what kind of ship it was. In port in Marseille the crew went ashore with money in their pockets. They bought new clothes and spent nights in the nightclubs. The wages were high but not that high. One night at sea a German crewman came to my cabin.

"You want to make extra money?" he asked.

"How?"

"Come with me."

I followed him down to the hold. Three other crew members were there with torches and had opened several crates marked for Casablanca. Inside were cases of French wine and cigarettes. They were taking out bottles and cartons and putting them in empty crates marked for ship's stores.

"We sell it in North Africa," the German said. "The manifest says it was damaged at sea. The captain gets his share. Everyone gets paid."

"What if we're caught?"

"We won't be. The captain handles the paperwork. In Casablanca you can sell anything for any currency. Cash, sterling, francs, whatever you want."

I needed money. I was banned from England and couldn't see my children. To hire a lawyer in France to fight the deportation order would cost more than I had. So, I helped them move the cargo and on the next run to Casablanca I went ashore with goods to sell. The dock workers knew what to buy and where to sell it. They took their cut and paid me in French francs. It was good money. We did this on every voyage. The captain knew. The whole crew knew. Nobody talked about it except among us. In port we spent freely and nobody asked questions.

We made several runs between France and North Africa. The money was good. I was saving to hire a lawyer. On the third day in Le Havre a telegram came to the ship. The captain brought it to me while I was working below decks.

"Someone in Finland is looking for you," he said.

The telegram was from Helmi in Mäntyluoto. It gave a telephone number and said to call. I went to the post office at the port and placed the call. A woman answered in Finnish. Then in English she said to call back in an hour. I walked along the docks and had coffee at a café. When I called again Helmi answered.

"How did you find me?" I asked.

"I work for shipping agent now," she said in broken English. "I see manifests. Your ship in Le Havre sometime."

"How is your mother?" I asked.

There was a pause. Then she laughed. "She good. Asking about you."

"Why are you calling?"

"I see Klaus in Copenhagen. German from your ship. He says you work good."

Klaus was the crewman who had brought me into the cargo operation and had left the ship in Copenhagen two weeks before.

"What does Klaus want?" I asked.

"He work now here. We have business in Finland. Shipping business." She paused. "We need someone speak Spanish. Klaus say you are good."

"What kind of business?"

"Great business. We trading with Vigo and A Coruña. Franco make Spain poor. Everything expensive and hard to find. We bring things they not have."

I understood what she meant. Smuggling into Spain. Franco had closed the borders. Spain made nothing and imported nothing. Everything was scarce. Everything was expensive. There was money in bringing things people needed or wanted.

"Why me?" I asked.

"You speak Spanish. You know ports. Klaus says you smart and keep mouth shut."

"What's the pay?"

"Better than now for you. You will live in Finland. I have place in Pori now. You stay with me."

It was a good offer. Better money than the Norwegian freighter. And Spain—I knew those ports. I could speak to the dock workers and the customs men in my own language.

"How would I get into Spain?" I asked. "Franco's men are looking for Republicans."

"Have French papers for you," she said. "Good papers. You travel like Frenchman. In port, speak Spanish to dock workers only. Private. Not police or customs. Understand?"

"I would need to hide that I'm Spanish?"

"Yes. Franco spies everywhere. They know you Republican, you disappear. So. You French sailor speaking little Spanish. That all."

I thought about it. Going back to Spain under a false name. Walking the docks of Vigo where I had walked as a young man. Speaking my own language in whispers. Hiding from Franco's police in my own country.

"No. I can't," I said.

There was silence on the line.

"Why no?" she asked. "You smuggler now. Same work. Better pay."

I didn't have a good answer. It was the same kind of work I was already doing. The false papers were no different from the forged seaman's documents I had used before. But going back to Spain as a ghost, as a Frenchman in my own country—something in me resisted. And living with Helmi and her mother in Finland, that life—I had tried settling down before. It never worked.

"I need to stay with this ship," I said.

"How long?"

"I'm saving money. For a lawyer. For my children."

"Money better than ship," she said. "You have money more fast."

"I know."

Another pause. Then she said something in Finnish that I didn't understand. When she spoke again in English her voice was different.

"You not want stop," she said. "You moving always, you not know how stop."

She was probably right. I had been moving from port to port for more than ten years. I had used false papers and false names in half a dozen countries. I had stolen cargo and paid bribes and watched for police in every port. I was tired of it, but I didn't know how to do anything else. And the thought of going back to Spain—even in disguise, even for money—felt like going backwards into something I had escaped.

" You change thinking. Call me," she said, and hung up.

I walked back to the ship. We sailed for North Africa the next morning but at sea the captain called us together. The orders had changed. We were going to Tenerife in the Canary Islands.

Spain. Franco's Spain. Again.

I had been to Tenerife once before on a different ship. There had been two of us Spaniards aboard that time. When the police came, they grilled us about politics. I told the officer we only talked about women and he laughed and let us through. The other Spaniard stayed on the ship the whole time, afraid to go ashore. But that was luck. This time I was traveling alone as a Spaniard on a Norwegian ship. I had never done military service under Franco and every Spanish man was supposed to serve. The regime kept records. I didn't know if the joke about women would work twice.

When we anchored at Santa Cruz de Tenerife, the police came aboard before we could unload. They checked papers for every crewman. A Guardia Civil officer looked at my French seaman's documents.

"You were born in Spain," he said in Spanish.

"Yes. But I left in 1939."

"Did you complete military service?"

"I served France in World War II."

"That doesn't count for Spain," he cut back.

I looked at him. "I'm not serving Franco for pennies."

There was a pause. The other crew members were watching. Then the officer snorted.

"Smart man," he said. He stamped my papers and handed me a shore pass. "Don't make trouble ashore."

I took the pass and went down to the dock. My hands were shaking.

Tenerife was beautiful. I had money in my pocket from the smuggling runs. It felt good to be ashore with cash. I had known a woman in Madrid during the Civil War. Her name was Carmela. I must have been about fourteen when we met and she was nineteen. We were close before the war ended. After Franco won, she married a colonel in the Spanish Foreign Legion. I heard she had moved to Tenerife. I found her name in the telephone directory at a café. There was an address and took a bus to her neighbourhood.

On the bus a boy sat across from me. He was about twelve or thirteen and kept staring. I looked out the window but I could feel his eyes on me. When I got off the bus, the boy got off too.

"Are you looking for someone?" he asked in Spanish.

"Maybe," I said.

"Who?"

"A woman named Carmela. She's married to a colonel."

The boy looked at me carefully. "That's my mother," he said. "Come with me."

He led me through narrow streets to a white house with blue shutters. We went inside. Carmela and her husband were happy to see me. We talked about the war and the years after. The colonel was polite. He poured wine, the boy sat at the table and watched me. In the afternoon Carmela walked me to the door while her husband and the boy stayed in the back room.

She leaned close. "That boy," she said. "He's your son."

The street tilted. I put my hand on the doorframe.

"Are you all right?" she asked.

"Yes."

"I wanted you to know. He doesn't know. My husband thinks he's his."

I looked back toward the house. Through the window I could see the boy's silhouette.

"Does he look like me?" I asked.

"Yes," she said. "Very much."

I walked back to the port. My legs felt heavy. At the ship I sat on my bunk and stared at the wall. Another child. Another child I would never know. We loaded tomatoes for London. Tomatoes bound for England. I would be close to my other children again. The ones I had raised until they were taken. I thought about jumping ship in Dover. Finding my wife's boyfriend, the man who had blackmailed me. I could find him. I knew where he lived.

The captain came to my cabin the night before we sailed.

"You've been quiet," he said.

"I'm not in control of myself anymore," I said.

"What are you talking about?"

I didn't answer. He waited. Then he sat down on the bunk across from me.

"Tell me," he said.

I told him about Tenerife. About the woman I knew during the Civil War. About the boy on the bus. About learning I had a son I would never know.

"That's four children now," I said. "Three in England I can't see. One in Tenerife I just learned about."

The captain listened without speaking.

"We're loading tomatoes for London," I said. "I'll be close to my children again. The ones in England. I keep thinking about jumping ship in Dover. Finding my wife's boyfriend. The man who blackmailed me. I know where he lives."

"What would you do if you found him?"

"I don't know."

The captain stood up and looked at me for a long moment.

"You're not going back to London," he said. "I'll arrange a transfer. Another ship on a different route."

"I signed on for this voyage."

"I'll handle it."

He left and I sat in the cabin and stared at the wall.

The next morning the captain called me to his cabin. There was a man with him in a suit. He was not a sailor.

"This is Mr. Patterson from the Home Office," the captain said.

Without looking at me, the man opened a folder.

"Alfonso Mora," he said. "Spanish national. Deported from England in 1949. You've violated the terms of your deportation by entering British waters multiple times since then."

"I work on ships," I said. "Ships go where they're ordered."

"You're to be transferred to a French vessel departing from Dover. The French authorities have agreed to accept you and you're banned from British territorial waters indefinitely."

I looked at the captain. His face was expressionless.

"When?" I asked.

"Tomorrow," Patterson said. "We arrive at six, the French ship sails at eight."

Around dawn I gathered my things. The captain came to my cabin.

"I had to report it," he said. "When you told me you were thinking of jumping ship, of finding that man. I couldn't let you do that."

"I understand."

"The French ship is a good one. Going to Marseille."

"All right."

"I'm sorry about your children."

I nodded and we shook hands.

Two men from the Home Office escorted me down the gangway and we walked to the French ship berthed beside ours. It was smaller, older. A cargo vessel. Walking across the wharf with my bag, behind me was England. My children were somewhere in that grey morning, and I didn't turn around.

Marseille was hot and bright after the English fog. I had money from the Norwegian ship, not much, but enough for a room and food for a few weeks. I found a cheap hotel near the Vieux Port. The room had a bed and a sink. That was all. At night I could hear the harbor through the thin walls. I had nowhere to go, no papers to work in France legally, no way back to England. Spain was still Franco's. My children were scattered across other countries, and I couldn't reach any of them.

I walked the docks looking for ships. Looking for anything. Just looking.

On the third day I passed a woman sitting at a small table on the street. She had cards laid out in front of her. A sign said "Fortunes - 10 francs." I had nothing else to do. I sat down and gave her ten francs. She shuffled the cards without looking at me. Then she laid them out in rows. She studied them for a long time.

"You've travelled far," she said in French.

"Yes."

"You have children."

"Yes."

"They're far away. You can't reach them."

I didn't say anything.

She touched one of the cards. "You will travel farther. Much farther. Years in distant lands. Hot lands. You won't return to Europe for a long time."

"How long?"

She shook her head. "I don't see. Many years."

She gathered up the cards. "That's all I can tell you."

I walked back to my hotel. The room felt smaller than before.

My money was running out. I had been in Marseille for three weeks. The room cost five francs a night. I had enough for maybe four more days.

I walked past the Foreign Legion recruitment office twice before I went in. It was on Rue des Catalans near the old port. The sign said "Légion Étrangère - Engagements."

Inside, a sergeant sat behind a desk. He was older, maybe fifty, with scars on his face and hands. He looked at me without expression.

"You want to enlist?" he asked in French.

"I'm thinking about it."

"Where are you from?"

"Spain."

"Republican or Nationalist?"

"Republican."

He nodded. "We have many Spanish Republicans. Good soldiers."

"I'm twenty-seven," I said. "I have no military experience."

"We train everyone. Age limit is forty. You're young enough."

He pushed a form across the desk. "Five-year contract. You go to Indochina. The war there is bad. Many men don't come back."

"What's the pay?"

"Room, board, uniform. Small salary. After five years, you can apply for French citizenship."

I looked at the form. At the top it said "Anonymat - Vous pouvez vous engager sous un nom d'emprunt." You can enlist under an assumed name.

"Where would I train?"

"Aubagne first. Then Algeria and then Indochina."

I thought about it. Five years. Fighting in jungles I had never seen. For a country that wasn't mine. Against people I had no quarrel with.

"What's in Indochina?" I asked.

"War," the sergeant said. "Heat. Malaria. Viet Minh."

"And if you survive?"

"French citizenship. A pension. A new life."

I picked up the pen. Then I put it down.

"I need to think about it," I said.

"The office is open every day," the sergeant said. "But think fast. A man without papers, without money—you don't have many options."

I walked back to the harbor. He was right. I didn't have many options, but I couldn't sign that paper. Not for five years and not for a war that wasn't mine. What I needed was a ship. Any ship, going anywhere. The next morning once again I walked the docks, at dawn. Ships were loading and unloading. Cranes swung cargo. Men shouted in French and Arabic and languages I didn't recognize. I asked at every ship if they needed crew. Most didn't answer. Some laughed. One captain said, "You have papers?"

"Seaman's documents," I said. "French."

"Let me see them."

I showed him my forged documents. He looked at them and handed them back.

"These are no good," he said. "But I need an able seaman. We sail tomorrow for Saigon."

"Saigon?"

"Yes. Indochina. We carry supplies for the army. Medical equipment, ammunition, food. The run takes six weeks. We stop in Durban for fuel."

"What's the pay?"

"Two hundred francs a week. Plus meals."

It wasn't much. But it was enough.

"When do I start?"

"Be here at six tomorrow morning. We sail at eight."

I went back to my room and packed my bag. Everything I owned fit in one canvas sack. Two shirts. One pair of pants. A razor. A comb. My forged papers.

That night I couldn't sleep. I kept thinking about the fortune teller. "You will travel farther. Much farther. Years in distant lands. Hot lands." Indochina was a hot land. But the ship would only be there a few weeks. Then back to France. Maybe. Or maybe something else would happen. Maybe I would jump ship in Saigon. Or Durban. Or anywhere that wasn't here.

At five in the morning, I walked to the docks. The ship was called the Marie-Claire. Old and rust-streaked but the engines looked good. Other crew members were already aboard. None of them spoke to me. The captain saw me and nodded. "Mora?"

"Yes."

"Good. Report to the bosun. He'll show you your berth."

The bosun was a short man with tattoos on both arms. He showed me to a cabin below decks. Six bunks. The other five were already taken.

"You're in the top bunk," he said. "Breakfast at six. We cast off at eight."

I climbed into the bunk and lay on my back. The ceiling was two feet above my face. I could hear the water against the hull, men talking in the corridor, and the ship's engines starting up. I was leaving Europe. Maybe for good. Maybe forever. The fortune teller had said years. I didn't believe in fortune tellers. But I believed in this ship. It was going somewhere far away and that was enough. At eight o'clock we cast off. I stood on deck and watched Marseille disappear behind us. The last piece of Europe I would see for a long time. I was twenty-seven years old. I had lived in Spain, France, England. I had fought in a war. I had married and lost everything. I had four children I would probably never know. I had been deported, arrested, blackmailed, and broken.

Now I was sailing away from all of it. Into what, I didn't know. But the fortune teller had been right. Years in distant lands. Hot lands. The ship's engines throbbed beneath my feet. The sea stretched empty ahead and I went below and reported for duty.

We unloaded medical supplies in Saigon. The heat was unbearable, and the harbor smelled of something I couldn't name. French soldiers were everywhere, and the war was going badly for them. You could see it in their faces. The captain warned us not to go into the city though we stayed three days. Some of the crew went anyway. I stayed on the ship. I had no reason to see Saigon. It wasn't my war.

On the second night a French officer came aboard. He was looking for men willing to sign on for transport work between Saigon and the forward bases. Good pay, he said.

Danger pay. I told him I wasn't interested. I had been running in and out of wars my whole life and I wasn't going to run toward one now.

From Vietnam we sailed for Durban to refuel, then we were scheduled to head back to Europe. Three weeks across the Indian Ocean with hot days and hotter nights. The crew was mostly French and North African. Nobody spoke Spanish. I hadn't spoken Spanish in months. Not since Tenerife. I missed it. Missed speaking plainly without translating my thoughts first. The crew kept to themselves, nobody talked much. We were all running from something. In Durban we took on coal and water. I stood on deck and looked at South African coast. I had never been this far south. The city looked clear from the harbor. White buildings against brown hills. A sailor asked if I was going ashore and I said no. He said there were women if you knew where to look. I said I wasn't interested.

"What are you interested in?" he asked.

I didn't have an answer.

We sailed from Durban heading east. The captain called the crew together once again. He said the Marie-Claire had new orders. We weren't going back to France, we were going to Australia. Sydney. To pick up wool and wheat for the return voyage.

"Anyone who wants to leave the ship in Sydney can do so," he said. "No questions asked. But you're on your own after that."

Australia. I had never thought about Australia. It was the other side of the world. As far from Spain as you could get. As far from England. As far from my children. As far from anywhere.

Maybe that was the point.

We left South Africa, heading east for Singapore before going for Sydney. Crossing the Indian Ocean, we entered the

Tasman Sea. The water was rougher here. Cold currents from the south. At night I stood at the rail and watched the stars. Different stars than in Europe. The Southern Cross low on the horizon.

One of the crew, a man from Algeria stood beside me mixing French and English.

"Getting off in Sydney?" he asked.

"I don't know."

"I will," he said. "They need workers in Australia. Good money and no questions."

"What kind of work?"

"Factory. Farm. Anything. After the war many immigrants. Many Europeans. They need men for work."

"You have papers?" I asked.

"I get papers," he said. "They don't care where you're from in Australia. Just care about work."

He walked away while I stayed at the rail. Australia. Hmm. A country I knew nothing about though as a joke I did claim to be one once. So it was a place where they didn't ask questions? Where they needed workers. Where I could disappear completely.

The next morning, we entered Port Jackson. Sydney spread out around the harbor. Bigger than I expected. Cleaner too. The water was blue and clear, and ships crowded the wharves.

We docked at Woolloomooloo at wharf number six.

PART II

Australia

14

ANCHORED AT WOOLLOOMOOLOO

At the wharf I was painting the hull when I heard Spanish from a nearby American ship, the Pioneer Sea. Hearing my own   language so far from home felt strange and good. "Are you Spanish?" I called. "No, Puerto Rican," they said. They invited me aboard for coffee and later to meet local women. I thanked them and said no. Paying for company wasn't my way. But the Puerto Ricans told me about other Spanish speakers in Sydney. South Americans mostly. Argentines, Chileans, a few Colombians. Working construction, loading docks, painting ships. Over the next weeks I found them. In bars near the waterfront. At boarding houses in Woolloomooloo, Kings Cross and Darlinghurst. Men like me—exiles, refugees, wanderers. With them I could talk straight. And in that plain talk I began to want steadier things: a room of my own, regular work, a life that didn't end with the next sailing. But we bonded well and they urged me to come with them to New York.

"There's work in New York," one of them said. "Good money. You speak Spanish, you'll find your people."

"I'll think about it."

But I wasn't going to New York. I had left enough places. I was tired of leaving. Their ship sailed for the States two days later. I watched it go from the wharf while the Puerto Ricans waved from the deck. I waved back. Then they were gone and I was alone again.

The Marie-Claire was scheduled to return to France in three weeks. I could stay aboard or I could jump ship. The captain had said no questions asked. But if I jumped, I would need work. Money. Papers. I walked into the city one afternoon, up from the wharves into the busy streets. Sydney was bigger than I expected. Trams running, cars and people everywhere. It was summer here. Hot and the sunlight stronger than I had seen. I heard music from an open door, a dance hall, and I went in.

After the bright street, it was dark inside. A band played on a small stage while a few couples danced. Others sat at tables drinking beer and the place was half empty. In one corner a woman sat alone. She was maybe thirty with dark hair and had her hands folded on the table in front of her. She wasn't drinking, wasn't watching the dancers. She was just sitting.

I bought a beer at the bar and stood watching. The woman didn't move. There was something about the way she sat. The stillness. Like she had nowhere to go.

I knew that feeling.

I walked over to her table. I knew what I was doing. I had seen lonely women before and I had been a lonely man for years.

"Would you like to dance?" I asked.

She looked up. "You're the first who has asked."

"Then let's dance."

We danced while the band played slow songs. She held on carefully, like she hadn't danced in a long time. Or like she was afraid I would let go. When the song ended, we sat at her table.

"My name is Alfonso," I said.

"Margaret."

We talked. The usual questions. Where are you from. What brought you here. How long are you staying. I told her the basics. Spain. The ship. Two weeks in port.

"Will you go back to France?" she asked.

"Probably."

"You don't sound sure."

"I'm not sure of anything," I said.

She smiled a little. "Neither am I."

We danced again. When the band stopped, it was late, and I walked her home. She lived in a small house in Woolloomooloo on a working class street not far from the wharves. I knew that kind of neighbourhood. I had lived in places like that most of my life.

At her door she said, "Would you like to come for dinner tomorrow? Sunday."

I should have said no. I had said no to women before but I was tired of saying no.

"What time?"

"Six o'clock."

She wrote the address on a piece of paper. I walked back to the ship knowing I probably shouldn't go though I knew I would anyway.

I put on my good shirt the next day and walked to her house. She answered the door in a different dress, her hair was done up. She had tried. So, had I.

"Come in," she said.

The house was clean but worn. Furniture that had seen better days and photos on the walls. Two children in the photos.

"Your children?" I asked.

"Yes. Peter and Susan. They're with their father this weekend."

I didn't ask more. I knew about separated parents, and I knew about children who weren't there.

She had made roast lamb. It was good. We ate and talked. She told me she was getting divorced after two years of paperwork. Her husband drank and hit her, so she took the children and left. Now he wanted custody, but he said she was unfit.

"Are you?" I asked.

She looked at me. "No."

"Then you'll be all right."

"I don't know," she said. "The courts favour fathers. Even ones who drink."

I knew about that too. About systems that didn't care what was right.

After dinner we sat in the sitting room and she made tea.

"What about you?" she asked. "You have children?"

"Three. In England. I haven't seen them in three years."

"Why not?"

"I was deported. I'm not allowed back."

"For what?"

"For being there illegally."

She nodded. "Do you miss them?"

"Every day."

We sat in silence as the clock ticked. Outside, someone walked past on the street.

"You could stay here," she said. "In Australia. Start over."

"I've started over before. It never works."

"Maybe this time is different."

"It never is," I said.

But I was lying. Part of me wanted it to be different. Part of me was tired of leaving. Tired of running. Tired of being alone.

I went with her to the Immigration office anyway. Not because I believed it would work, but because she asked and I had nothing to lose. Her friend worked there as a secretary. She looked at my French seaman's papers and frowned.

"You're Spanish but you have French documents?"

"Yes."

"And you want to stay in Australia?"

"I'm considering it."

She looked at Margaret, then back at me. "Without proper papers, you'd need to apply for refugee status. Or get an employer to sponsor you. Both take months. If your ship leaves in two weeks, you'd have to jump ship and stay illegally."

"What happens if I'm caught?"

"Deportation, probably back to Spain."

Spain. Franco's Spain. That wasn't an option for me.

"What if I don't get caught?"

"Then you work under the table. Cash jobs. Don't use your real name. Don't get arrested. Don't draw attention."

I had lived that way before. In England and in France. Maybe I could do it again.

"I'll think about it," I said.

Outside, Margaret said, "You're going to do it, aren't you?"

"I don't know."

"Yes, you do," she said. "You're going to jump ship."

She was right. I was going to do it. Not because I believed it would work out but because I had nowhere else to go. And because she was there. And because I was weary.

Two weeks later the Marie-Claire sailed for Adelaide. I went with her and worked my shifts. I kept quiet. The captain didn't suspect anything. Why would he? I was just another seaman. In Adelaide I met a Mexican at the Seamen's Mission in Todd Street. His name was Robert and was the chief electrician on the Monte Rey. We sat drinking coffee, and he asked where I was headed.

"I'm jumping ship," I said. "Going back to Sydney."

"A woman?"

"Yes."

He nodded. "Adelaide's not bad if you need work. But Sydney's bigger. More places to disappear."

"That's the idea."

"Good luck," he said. "Don't get caught."

The next morning I walked off the ship with my bag. Nobody stopped me. The Marie-Claire sailed without me and I took a train back to Sydney, changing trains at the Victorian border. Margaret met me at Central Station. When she saw me, she smiled. Not a big smile. Just a small one. Like she hadn't been sure I'd come back.

"You came," she said.

"I said I would."

"Men say a lot of things."

"I know," I said. "But I'm here."

We walked out of the station together. I had jumped ship in a foreign country with forged papers and no legal status. Again. But this time felt different. Not because I believed it would work. But because I was choosing to stay instead of being forced to leave.

That had to count for something.

We spent the weekend together. Saturday and Sunday night. Monday morning she made breakfast and I could tell something was wrong.

"My husband called," she said. "He wants to come back."

I put down my coffee. "What did you tell him?"

"I said I'd think about it." She looked at me. "What should I do?"

"Has he stopped drinking?"

"He says he has."

"And you believe him?"

"No."

"Then you know the answer."

She sat down across from me. "But the children need their father."

"The children need their mother alive. If he hit you before, he'll hit you again."

"Maybe it will be different this time."

"It won't be. Men like that don't change. You know that already."

She was quiet. Then she said, "But I can't make it alone. The courts will give him custody if I can't support them. I need his income."

"What about your friend at Immigration? Could she help you find work?"

"Maybe. But it takes time, and he wants an answer now."

I thought about it. She was trapped. I knew that feeling.

"You could refuse him," I said. "Tell him no. Keep the children away from him."

"He'll go to court. He'll tell them I'm unfit, that I go to dance halls. That I... that I have men over."

"Do you have family?"

"My sister. But she has her own problems. She can't take us in."

"What about the police? You could report him. File charges for assault."

She laughed bitterly. "The police don't care. It's a domestic matter. They told me that when I called them before. They said marriage is between husband and wife. They said I should try to work it out."

I knew she was right. I had seen it before. In England. In Spain. Everywhere. The authorities didn't protect women from their husbands.

"Then you have three choices," I said. "You can go back to him and hope he's changed, knowing he probably hasn't. You can refuse him and risk losing your children in court. Or you can run. Take the children and disappear."

"Where would I go?"

"I don't know. But there are places. Women's shelters. Churches. Your friend at the Immigration Office might know."

She shook her head. "If I run, he'll find me and then it will be worse."

We sat in silence. The clock ticked. Outside, someone walked past on the street.

"I think I have to go back," she said finally.

"You don't have to."

"Yes, I do. For the children. I can keep him calm if I'm careful. I know what sets him off. I can manage him."

" You shouldn't have to manage him."

"But I do. That's the reality." She looked at me. "You understand reality. That's why I asked you. You don't lie to make things easier."

"The reality is that he might kill you one day."

"Maybe. But if I don't go back, I'll lose my children for certain. I'd rather take the risk."

I wanted to tell her she was wrong. But I couldn't. She was right about the courts. Right about the police. Right about her choices.

"If you go back," I said, "you need a plan. Money hidden away. A bag packed. Somewhere to run if it gets bad. You can't just hope for the best."

"I will."

"Promise me. If he hits you again, you take the children and leave. Don't wait. Don't think about it. Just go."

"Where?"

"Tell your friend I sent you to her. Tell her you need help. She'll know people. Churches, charities. Someone will help."

"All right."

"Promise me."

"I promise."

But I knew she probably wouldn't leave. Most women didn't. They stayed until it was too late. I had seen it before.

I left that afternoon and at the door she touched my arm.

"Thank you for being honest," she said. "And for caring. Most wouldn't."

"I don't want you to get hurt."

"I know. But this is the choice I'm making. For my children."

"I understand. But the offer stands. If you need to leave, come find me. I'll help however I can."

"You won't be here. You're illegal. You'll be hiding too."

"Then we'll both be hiding. But the offer stands."

She kissed me on the cheek. "Good luck."

"You too and keep safe."

I was alone in Sydney. No job. No ship. No legal status. Turning myself in meant jail for deserting the ship. I needed work fast. I had about fifteen pounds left from my wages, which would last two weeks if I was careful. I needed work before the money ran out. I spent three days walking the docks looking for ships that would take me on with my papers. None would. I tried the factories in Pyrmont and Ultimo. They wanted references. Work papers. Things I didn't have.

On the fourth day I had to sleep in Hyde Park alongside a few hobos, but the police moved us on at dawn. I asked other men on the street where to find work, cash work with no questions. They told me to try the pubs in Darlinghurst and Surry Hill. Ask the bartenders. They knew people. I tried five pubs but most bartenders ignored me or told me to leave.

At the sixth pub, a woman sitting at the bar overheard me and when the bartender walked away, she said, "You need money?"

"I need work."

"Same thing." She looked me over. "You're foreign."

"Spanish."

"You got papers?"

"No."

She smiled. "Then you're in trouble, aren't you?"

Her name was Betty and she worked in the infamous part of Forbes Street. She knew people who hired men like me. Men who couldn't go to the labour exchange. But she wanted something first.

"Twenty pounds," she said. "I make some calls; I get you work. Twenty pounds."

I had fifteen. I told her.

"Fifteen then. And you owe me the rest when you get paid."

I gave her the money, which she could have just taken and disappear. But she didn't. She made the calls right there from the pub phone. When she came back, she wrote an address on a piece of paper.

"Exide Batteries at Camperdown. Ask for Mr. Patterson. Seven tomorrow morning and tell him Betty sent you. Cash pay. Six pounds a week."

"What about a place to stay?"

"That costs extra. Five more pounds when you have it, then I'll get you a room."

I worked at Exide for a week. The work was brutal, but the money was real. At the end of the week I found Betty at the same pub and gave her five pounds. She took me to a boarding house in Woolloomooloo. The landlord was an Italian greengrocer named Sal. His shop was on the ground floor and the rooms upstairs. Sal was a cheat. His scales were rigged. His arithmetic was creative. In his math, two plus two equalled eight. But he was decent enough in his own way and didn't ask questions or call Immigration. And Betty had vouched for me, which apparently counted for something in this part of Sydney.

The house was old. Gas lamps. Strange noises at night. The other tenants said it was haunted. Maybe it was, but the rent was cheap and I could afford it. I lived there eight months. Men came and went. Italians, Greeks, Poles, Irish. All of us running from something. All of us illegal or close to it. We didn't become friends, but sometimes at night we sat in the kitchen and shared what we had. Sal would come up with a bottle of grappa, and we'd drink and talk about nothing important by warm light of the gas lamps. Those nights weren't much. Yet they were enough. It was the first time since leaving England that I had something like a home.

Not far from Sal's shop stood Saint Mary's Cathedral. Every Sunday morning, he went to mass. Every other day, he cheated everyone who walked through his door. His scales were rigged. I watched him weigh out a pound of tomatoes for an old woman. When she left, I bought a pound of tomatoes. He used the same scale, but my pound weighed less. I said nothing. I needed the room upstairs.

He sold day-old bread as fresh. He picked through the fruit and sold the good pieces to Australians. The bruised fruit went to immigrants who couldn't complain. If you bought on credit, he added twenty percent interest and then he rounded up to the nearest shilling. By Friday my pay was gone. By Monday I was asking him for credit. He'd write it down in his book with a smile. He knew I had no choice.

"Two plus two equals eight," he'd say when he totalled the accounts. He thought it was funny.

But he never called Immigration. He never asked questions. He let us live upstairs when no one else would.

That was worth something. Maybe that's what he asked forgiveness for on Sunday mornings. Or maybe he just liked the grand cathedral.

On Friday nights after work, I went to the Italo-Australian Club on George Street, a meeting place for mostly young Italian men. A place to eat Italian food and speak the language. I wasn't Italian but they let me in. Spanish was close enough. Spanish speakers were scarce in Sydney. I found six. Two were South American. The rest were Spanish like me. We'd sit at a corner table and drink red wine and talk.

The fifties brought many new immigrants. Italians mostly. Greeks. Some Spanish. The men would complain about Australian women. Too independent. Too expensive. Too demanding. They'd court them for months without spending money. Then they'd save enough to bring a bride from home. A proper woman who knew how to behave. The local women figured it out soon enough. They stopped going out with immigrants. Called us cheap. Called us users. They weren't wrong.

I didn't do that. I had no money to bring anyone from anywhere. And I already had a wife in England I couldn't divorce. But I watched the other men do it. Watched them string along Australian girls while saving for tickets home. It wasn't right. But I said nothing. We were all trying to survive. We all did what we had to do. Still, I thought I was different from the other immigrants. I wasn't saving for a ticket home. I wasn't looking for a bride. I lived day to day. Paycheck to paycheck.

One afternoon walking home from work along Bourke Street, someone whistled. A woman on a porch across the street. She was young, pretty and well-dressed but She looked at me like I was something curious.

"You speak Spanish?" she called out.

"Yes," I said and started to walk on.

"I thought so." She called back. "You know a Mexican lives here?"

I stopped. "Where?"

"This house. My brother-in-law." She said it without much interest, as if she were bored and I was just something to look at.

A man came to the door behind her. He was olive skinned and about my age.

"Jean, who are you talking to?" Then he saw me and smiled. "Alfonso?"

It was Robert. The chief electrician from the Monte Rey. The one I'd met in Adelaide at the Seamen's Mission.

"You know him?" Jean asked, surprised.

"We met in Adelaide," Robert said. "Come in, Alfonso. Tell me how you've been surviving."

Jean went inside ahead of us without another word. She had been dating a businessman, a gym owner that Robert told me about later. A well-off man who bought her expensive things and took her to restaurants I could never afford. She had a three-year-old boy named Paul. I didn't know her story then. I learned it later, after we were together, after she trusted me enough to tell it. She had been eighteen when she got pregnant, just a girl really, and when she was eight months along her mother had a stroke and died in her arms. She held her mother while she died and a month later, she had the baby alone. That kind of thing marks a person. It explained some things about her—a certain hardness, the way she kept people at a distance, the businessman with his money who could never really reach her.

I was a poor immigrant living in a room with holes in the walls, and I thought that she had no interest in men like me, that the whistle was just something to do on a slow afternoon, a way to pass the time and feel noticed. Maybe she was bored with the businessman and his money. Maybe she just liked the attention. I didn't know then that she would become my wife, that I would adopt Paul and raise him as my own, that we would build a life together in that broken-down neighbourhood.

"I'm here now, married to an Australian girl. I jumped ship. Like you. Tell me. What about you?" Robert asked.

He invited me in for dinner and his family was warm and his wife easy to talk to. He lived in that house. It was clean and comfortable. More than I had. Jean, his sister-in-law sat at the table and listened then told us she was having a party that weekend.

"You should come," Robert said.

"I don't know anyone."

"You know us. That's enough."

"All right then. I'll bring wine," I said.

The night of the party I bought two bottles of Penfolds. Cheap red. Three shillings a bottle. When I arrived with them, Jean looked at the bottles and then at me.

"How thoughtful," she said in a flat voice.

The other guests had brought more expensive wine. French and Italian bottles. Champagne. My Penfolds looked like what they were. Poor man's wine.

"It's what I can afford," I said.

"Of course." She took the bottles and put them on a side table, away from the other wine.

But the party was good. Robert introduced me to people, businessmen, promoters. Jean sang. She had a real voice. Trained. She knew people from the theatre. One man talked about Harry M. Miller, the Australian producer. Another talked about American boxers coming to Australia for exhibition fights. I told stories about Spain and about bullfighting, boasting about my time in the ring. I told about working on ships and about my family in England. People listened, asking questions. By the end of the night, we'd finished two bottles of the expensive French wine and an Italian bottle. No one had touched my Penfolds.

After most of the guests left, I sat in the kitchen with Robert and Jean came in.

"You're different from what I expected," she said.

"What did you expect?"

"Another poor immigrant. Ashamed. Trying to pretend you're something you're not."

"I'm not ashamed."

"I can see that." She picked up one of my bottles of Penfolds. "This is actually quite good, you know. Better than most people realize."

She poured three glasses. We drank together and it tasted the same as usual. Maybe better.

A few weeks later I saw an advertisement in the paper. The Young Spring Festival Carnival was looking for volunteers. New event. New festival. I'd been in Sydney eight months, and the city was beginning to feel familiar. Like something I understood, so I applied for work at the Spring Carnival.

They hired me!

But Robert had other ideas for me. Bullfighting could be the next big show in Australia. A spectacle. Something new. No one had ever seen it here. He'd gone to the Sun newspaper without telling me. I found out when I came home from work. Reporters waiting outside my boarding house. Five of them. Cameras. Notebooks.

"You're the bullfighter?" one asked.

"Who told you that?"

"Your friend. Robert. Says you fought in Spain."

I looked at Robert standing behind them. He smiled like he'd done something good.

"It's a great story," he said. "Australia's never seen a bullfight. They want to write about you."

The flashes went off. I couldn't see for a moment. Then they were asking questions. Where did I fight? How many bulls? Was I famous in Spain? I answered because I couldn't leave. They were blocking the door. The story ran on Sunday. Front page. SPANISH BULLFIGHTER IN SYDNEY. They'd made me sound more important than I was. I'd fought a few bulls, yes. But I wasn't a matador. I was mostly a banderillero. A support man. But the paper didn't care about details.

Two days later Robert came to see me.

"They want to do it," he said. "A real bullfight. Here in Sydney. You could organize it."

"I can't organize a bullfight."

"Why not? You know how it's done."

"I know how to fight a bit. That's different from organizing."

"But you could learn. They'll pay you. Good money."

I thought about it. I was making six pounds a week at the battery factory. My hands were scarred from the acid. A bullfight might pay twenty. Maybe thirty pounds.

"When?" I asked.

"A month. Maybe six weeks."

"That's not enough time."

"It's what they're offering."

I agreed. I was a fool. But I needed the money.

The problem was finding men who knew what they were doing. I put the word out at the Italian club. Spanish speakers. Anyone from Spain. Finally, a Frenchman showed up. He'd never fought bulls, but he'd seen bullfights in the south of France. I hired him but had a lot to learn. I needed at least one more Spaniard. Someone who understood the culture. The ritual. I asked everyone at the club. No one wanted to do it. Then one Friday night a new man walked in, a young Spaniard. Well-dressed and he had money. You could tell by his shoes. Expensive leather. He drove a Packard. Black. New.

He'd just arrived in Sydney. Paid off from a ship. He had cash and no friends, and he was bored.

"You're organizing a bullfight?" he asked after someone told him.

"Yes."

"I'll help."

"You know bullfighting?"

"I'm from Andalusia. Everyone knows bullfighting."

"Have you fought?"

"No. But I've watched. That's enough, isn't it?"

It wasn't. But I had no choice.

"What's your name?"

"García."

"Why do you want to help?"

He shrugged. "Something to do. And I have a car. You'll need transportation, won't you?"

He was right. I needed his car more than I needed his knowledge of bullfighting, so we shook hands and he joined us. He'd drive and help however I needed. Later Robert told me García was tight with money. Mean with it. But he had what we needed. So, I kept him on. García had the Packard. I had the English. That's how we worked. I'd fill the car with women and friends from around Sydney. We'd drive to parks, beaches, restaurants. I did the talking. García did the driving.

"Tell them I own a shipping agency," he'd say.

"You want me to lie?"

"It's not lying. It's... translating."

But he spoke no English, and the women figured it out quickly. When they asked him questions and he couldn't answer, they'd look at me.

"He's just the driver," I'd say. "My assistant."

García would sit there smiling. Not understanding. Not knowing I'd demoted him.

One night a woman asked him directly. "What do you do?"

He looked at me. I shrugged. "Tell her yourself."

He tried. Broken English and hand gestures. She laughed. Not cruelly. But she laughed. He went red, got up and left the restaurant. In the car afterward he wouldn't speak to me.

"What did you tell them?" he finally asked in Spanish.

"That you're my driver."

"Your driver? I own this car. You own nothing."

"But I speak the language. They want to talk to me. Not you."

"Then find your own car."

But he didn't mean it. He had nowhere else to go and I needed the car.

The publicity kept growing. The newspapers loved the story. SPANISH BULLFIGHTERS IN SYDNEY. Robert arranged for us to do a demonstration in Young. A small country town in New South Wales full of country people. They'd never seen anything like it. We drove out there, set up the ring and practiced with a young bull. But the Royal Society for the Protection of Cruelty to Animals got word. They came with lawyers. Papers. Injunctions.

"You can't fight bulls in Australia," they said. "It's animal cruelty."

"It's culture," I said.

"It's illegal."

The show was cancelled. All that preparation. All that publicity. Gone. We drove back to Sydney with nothing.

García got quieter after that and stopped coming to the club and stopped calling. Then one day I saw him with a woman. She was much older than him, in her fifties at least.

But she had money and a house. She wanted company and he needed somewhere to live.

"She takes care of me," he said when I asked.

"And the Packard?"

"She doesn't like me driving it. Says it's wasteful."

Six months later he was gone. He just disappeared. Someone said that he'd left Sydney, that he couldn't take it anymore. The woman was jealous and controlling. She watched him constantly. He'd gone from owning a Packard to being a kept man who couldn't leave the house.

I never saw him again.

There were other Spaniards in Sydney then, and one had also married an Australian woman. He fancied himself a ladies' man. His wife was plain enough to empty a room, but he carried himself with the swagger of a man who had conquered continents. In the early days they lived frugally, counting every penny and eating tinned soup for dinner, but over time they built something and the money came. It was one of those immigrant stories Australia was full of back then, the kind where people arrived with nothing and clawed their way up. The man accumulated wealth and properties and a bank account that grew fat with zeros, but none of it changed who he was underneath. My father used to say you can dress a monkey in silk, and it remains a monkey, and watching this man proved the old saying true.

An American ship docked, and one of its crew came to visit Robert while I was there. He was a decent man, pleasant company, and we sat around talking for a while. I got distracted when Jean came into the room and on a whim, watching her from across the room, I asked her if she would like to come out dancing with me that night. To my surprise, she agreed. We arranged to meet at eight-thirty downtown, and I arrived on time and waited.

She didn't show.

I waited until ten o'clock, my anger building with each passing minute, and then I went to her home. She wasn't there. When she finally returned and saw me waiting on her doorstep, her face went pale. I had never raised my hand to a woman before that night, not in all my years, but standing there in the darkness I was frustrated and felt betrayed and I slapped her.

It seemed to bring her back to earth, or that's what I told myself then. Within a week we had started living together as if we were husband and wife. But looking back now, across all these years, I wonder what kind of man does such a thing. I wonder if what I called frustration was really just the old violence I'd learned in the war and on the ships, the same violence I'd seen in my grandfather when he raised his hand to my grandmother. You carry these things with you. They become part of who you are, and you don't always recognize them until it's too late, until you've already done the damage.

In those days, jobs were scarce without the right papers. The battery factory paid me enough for rent in King's Cross for Jean and I, and not much more. I found work on a city railway tunnel. They needed men who could handle dynamite. I learned as I went. The pay was better and reflected the danger. The foreman was Australian, of German descent. He walked through the tunnel with his chest out and his chin up. He spoke to the European workers the way a camp guard speaks to prisoners. Many of them had come from the camps. They knew that voice. He used it on me too. I tolerated it for weeks, biting down on my anger and doing the work. One day he pushed too far. I grabbed a shovel and walked toward him.

"Listen, you bastard," I said. "I served in the Second World War with the Free French and the Merchant Navy. I'm not from any camp and I won't take your abuse. So piss off."

He went white. The next day he left me alone. The day after that too. I kept my distance and watched him. I watched who he spoke to and how he spoke to them. I watched who he feared and who feared him. That told me what I needed to know about the tunnel and the men who worked there.

Now, Robert's sister-in-law, Jean, became my girlfriend, and her brother, Ozzie, also started work with me in the tunnel. We were at her family's place in Bourke Street one evening when Ozzie mentioned the foreman to her.

"Do you know who works as a foreman in the tunnel?" he said. "Our cousin Kalle."

I was stunned. It was the same man I had nearly hit with the shovel, the one who had gone white when I told him to piss off.

"If he's your cousin," I said, "I'd hate to meet the rest of your family."

The next day Kalle learned who I was dating and he started assigning me lighter tasks, easier work that wouldn't break a man's back. I paid him no mind and kept up with everyone else, doing the heavy work I was hired to do.

The pay was enough and we managed to save a bit each week, putting money aside for better times. But six months later the tunnel project shut down. The government had run out of money. They always did. Jobs dried up overnight. Men stood around the docks in the morning waiting for work that didn't come. The rent in King's Cross kept climbing and there was no work to pay it. So I went back to the greengrocer and asked if he had a room. He complained about rent and showed me a newspaper story about the Australian economy. There it was - inflation, wool prices printed in small numbers that kept getting bigger. He offered me a cramped space for five pounds a week. Twenty shillings to a pound—it was tight, but I took it and we moved back to Woolloomooloo. Those days Australia was a wild place where the big fish ate

the little fish and there wasn't much anyone could do about
it. Things don't seem to have changed much since then.
That's why there are so many millionaires here.

15

SAINTS, SNAKES, AND SPAGHETTI

Sydney was built by convicts—people like me. They were unlucky men and women forced to come here, and when their sentences ended, they had no money to return to Europe. So, they stayed and started families, like me. I don't regret it. Politically, Australia reminded me of Spain in some ways. In the thirties, Spain had a king who travelled the world while his people went hungry. The Spaniards threw him out and called it a republic. In Australia, there was Robert Menzies who spent more time in England than at home. Workers had no choice but to form unions. But some men turned even that noble idea into advantage for themselves.

We rented a one-bedroom place from Sal, the Italian greengrocer. It was a tiny terrace house on the lower end of Crown Street. An Italian family lived upstairs, and we had the ground floor. Sal's shop was a few houses away on the corner, and when we needed groceries, I could walk there in a minute. The room was big enough for the three of us at first. We had no television and nothing else to do, so we began making children in that little place. Our first was born right there. I named him Manolete, after the great matador who died in Linares before I left Spain. It was a good Spanish name, I thought, something he could carry with pride in this country where everyone was John or Bill or Bob. The Australians couldn't pronounce it. They called him Manuel or Manny or just gave up and made up anything. To me he was always Manolete.

The little place in Crown Street had air conditioning because the walls were full of cracks. It leaked when it rained and we joked about sleeping under umbrellas. We were downstairs and I couldn't imagine what the family upstairs was getting. But Sal never fixed the cracks. Too miserly. Lying there at night with the water dripping through the ceiling, I thought about the attic in Madrid where I grew up with my mother and sisters. That attic had the same holes in the walls and the same rain coming through. I had sailed halfway around the world, crossed oceans and continents, survived war and deportation, and ended up in the same place I started. But I remember the place fondly. The neighbourhood had rough men and women. Some on the wrong side of the law. Men who had done time, men who would do time again. Yet we slept with windows open. Maybe because there was nothing worth stealing. I used to think that even the rats felt sorry for us.

At six o'clock the bars closed. Men got off work at five. They had one hour to drink, and they made the most of it, downing beer after beer until the bartender called last orders. They always got drunk. It was good business for the government—the police collected them at closing time, locked them up for the night, and charged them ten shillings in the morning for their accommodation. Every afternoon Jean and I sat on the doorstep with Paul and watched the roundup. The police herded the drunks down the street like cattle being driven to market, and they loaded them onto the Black Maria, a big police truck, and drove them away to the station. It was entertainment in Woolloomooloo, better than the pictures and it didn't cost anything. Paul learning to count then, loved to total them—five drunks one day, eight the next, sometimes a dozen on Fridays when the men got paid.

In those days, almost everyone in Woolloomooloo was Australian. They were good people, always ready to help. There was a camaraderie you don't see anymore, a willingness to look out for your neighbours that felt natural back then. Mrs. Wilson had a house always full of visitors. She wouldn't let anyone leave without a cup of tea, though she was just a pensioner and had little to spare. Then there was my friend, Juan, another well-off Spaniard with his expensive suits and his Casanova ways. Once, when I was sick, he lent me ten pounds. I thought it was a gift, but when I got better, he came around every week with a little book, collecting ten shillings from me each time and writing it down in careful script. With all his money and all his properties, he was never happy.

Juan worked around the clock making money, but his wife gambled it away on horses and his daughter spent it touring the world. You had to feel sorry for the poor rich man. He was like a walking chemist shop, with tablets in his pockets for ears, nose, stomach, and God knows what else. He had come to Australia with nothing sixty years ago. Now he was a millionaire, but he was dying on his feet.

All of this happened in Woolloomooloo, yet despite the poverty and the drunks and the rough men, it was good living there. There was a warmth among the people, a willingness to help each other that reminded me of Spain before the war, when neighbours still looked after one another and no one locked their doors at night. In Woolloomooloo, we had nothing, but we had each other.

Because of the poor conditions in our house, Jean, my wife—we were practically married by then—developed asthma from the mold and dampness. Even so, three children were born there. Firstly, there was Paul, then Manolete, Cristina and Teresa. All of them in that small place with holes in the walls and leaking water. I found work as a welder in a glass factory. It kept us afloat, more or less, though the pay was never enough and the work was hard on the lungs. But Woolloomooloo never had a dull moment. Our bedroom was at the front door, and we had to lock it and enter from the street through the backyard, past the kitchen, stepping around beds everywhere because there was no space for anything else. The children slept wherever there was room, and at night the house was a maze of bodies and blankets. But we managed. We always managed.

The Brazilian Consul, Carlos Zalapa, was a good friend. Sometimes he helped me out with money when work was scarce. One day I told him I was illegal in Australia, that I had four kids and no papers, and I was afraid they would deport me. He listened, then picked up the phone and spoke to someone in English for a long time. When he hung up he told me to come back in two days. When I returned, he had papers for me to sign—applications, declarations, character references he had written himself. He told me to take them to York Street, to the Immigration Office, and to tell them I had been working as a welder for three years and had four Australian-born children. Don't volunteer anything else, he said. Just answer their questions.

I went the next day. The waiting room was full of people like me—Greeks, Italians, Yugoslavs, Germans—all of us waiting with our papers. When they called my name, I went into an office where a man looked at my forms and asked me questions about my work, about the children, about where I was living. He spoke slowly so I could understand. Then he stamped the papers and told me to come back in three months to collect my residency permit. That was all. After all those years of running and hiding and being illegal, I was going to be legal.

There weren't many Spanish speakers in Sydney in those days. When you heard Spanish on the street, you stopped. You introduced yourself. That's how I met Zalapa, the Migration and Visa Officer at the Brazilian Consulate. I was at a café on Liverpool Street, ordering coffee in Spanish—the owner was Spanish and it was the only place I knew where they understood me—and a man at the next table turned around. He was well-dressed, good suit and shoes. You're Spanish? he asked in Spanish. I said yes. He smiled and asked if he could join me.

We sat and talked for an hour, maybe more. He told me where he worked, and that he'd worked in Argentina for several years and spoke Spanish better than Portuguese. When he asked what I did, I told him I worked as a welder at a glass factory and lived in Woolloomooloo. He didn't seem to care about the class difference between us. We both spoke Spanish in a city where almost no one did, and that was enough. After that, we met every few weeks at the same café. Sometimes other Spanish speakers would join us—a Colombian Consulate worker, a few Argentines, a Chilean businessman. A few years later, that part of Liverpool Street became the Spanish quarter, but back then it was just a café where we could speak our language.

Later, Zalapa introduced me to Bernardo Jaramillo, one of the Colombian Consulate Secretaries. We got along well. He drove a late-model American car and lived in a big apartment in Kings Cross, but when we talked in Spanish about home, about politics, about the old country, the differences between us didn't matter much. Every now and then, I'd visit him at his apartment for a drink on Sunday afternoons. On one occasion, after we'd been talking for a couple of hours, I said I had to go. The wife will have lunch waiting. What are you having? he asked. Spaghetti, I said. I love spaghetti, he said, and before I could say anything else, he added, I'll come with you. I didn't know what to say. My place is nothing like this, I finally managed. He just smiled. I'm coming for lunch, not to buy your house.

We drove to Woolloomooloo in his new Ford. People stopped and stared—it was one of the first cars like that in the neighbourhood. We had to go in through the back door because the front bedroom was locked as usual. Jean was cooking. I brought the Secretary from the Colombian Consulate for lunch, I told her. She glared at me, then at him in his fancy clothes, then back at me. She didn't say a word, just turned back to the stove.

The kids had spaghetti on their shirts, on their faces, on the table. Jaramillo sat down and ate like he hadn't eaten in days. When he finished, he leaned back in his chair and said it was the best spaghetti he'd had in a long time. I don't know if he meant it. But it was a kind thing to say. Years later, he was posted to Belgium.

A few houses up the road lived an old Italian lady who knew Jean's father, Adolfo. She'd been in Australia since the First Fleet, or close to it. We invited her for tea sometimes in the afternoon. Her house looked like a church with pictures of saints everywhere, and she had a photo of the Pope on the wall. Right next to him was Stalin. She spent forty hours a week in church, but something told me not to trust her.

Down at the Woolloomooloo waterfront, ships from every country came through. That's how I met Jian, a Chinese seaman from a British ship who hailed from Canton. Every trip, he brought watches from Hong Kong. I'd take them to the glassworks where I worked, and someone else sold them. I made a pound profit on each watch. Not bad for something so small. I was making a few pounds, not much, but it kept the roof over our heads. Then one day, that old Italian witch came by again, the religious one who drank tea and stared too long at the walls. She was sitting in the kitchen, her hands wrapped around the cup, when the Chinese seaman came in through the back door with a parcel full of watches. He put the package on the table, right in front of her. Didn't think twice.

She finished her tea, said goodbye, and walked out. Something felt off. Maybe the way she didn't finish her biscuit. I took the watches to a mate's place, just to be safe. When I came back, the police were waiting. They said they wanted to search the place. I told them to go ahead. There was nothing to find. They didn't look pleased. That witch had tipped them off, I was sure of it. That was Woolloomooloo—most people would hand you their last crust, some would hand you to the cops.

A few months later, the glassworks shut down. I was out of work again, four kids to feed. But the neighbours were good. They gave what they could, even when they had nothing to spare themselves. Jean's Italian father, her sister and Italian husband lived just around the corner in Forbes Street. They never offered so much as a cup of tea. Strangers helped us more than her own blood.

Her father had money. One day I asked him for a loan—fifty pounds to take the family north, maybe find work in Queensland. He reached into his coat, pulled out a fat roll of notes, and said, I've got money, but I need it for myself. We'd argued before about the war in Spain. He'd said Mussolini did what he had to do. I'd said Mussolini helped Franco kill Spaniards. After that, we didn't talk much. I told myself, one day you'll pay for that. And he did.

Three months without work. Then the Sal the landlord called me in. "There's an old Spanish man in the shop. No family. Nowhere to go. Maybe you can help him." I went to the shop and saw the old man who looked like he hadn't eaten in days, hadn't shaved in weeks. His coat was expensive once, good wool, but worn through at the elbows. The room above us was vacant so without telling Sal, we took the old man in. My wife cleaned the room and made up a bed. Every day I bought him cigarettes and we fed him. He wouldn't let us wash his coat keeping it on even when he slept. He didn't say much, just sat and smoked and stared out the window. Sometimes he'd ask where he was. I'd tell him. He'd nod, but an hour later he'd ask again. This went on for a few weeks. Then one morning he seemed clearer and said he was going to Melbourne. Could you help me with my suitcases? he asked. I said sure. I picked up the first one and it nearly pulled me down the stairs. Careful, he said. There's twelve thousand pounds in that one. I set it down slowly. I'd been feeding a man who lived like a beggar and carrying a fortune in a suitcase. He was a sugar farmer from Queensland, he told me, though I don't know if he remembered telling me. He thanked me and left. My wife and I looked at each other. That was Woolloomooloo. You never knew.

Eventually, I got a job at Sargent's, the pie factory in Burton Street, Darlinghurst. They made the best meat pies in Sydney. Heavy things, full of meat and fat and steam. The kind of food that burned your mouth if you were too eager. The place smelled like flour and meat and boiled gravy. It was noisy in the day—banging trays, loud voices, trucks backing up to the loading docks. But at night, it went quiet. That's when I worked. The money wasn't good; it was steady but I should have asked for more.

Night shift suited me. I had the days to myself, and in my part of the factory I was mostly alone. No one watched me. I liked that and the regular money was welcome. The flour room where I worked was really big, a room where your footsteps echoed, even when you tried to walk soft. I'd be in there alone for hours. One night, I heard something move by the sacks. Not fast. Slow and heavy. I thought it was a rat. Maybe two. I went to check. It wasn't a rat, it was a snake.

It was dark and long, coiled like rope left out in the sun, and yellow diamonds ran down its back. It was two metres, easy. It looked at me without moving. So not thinking twice, I grabbed a shovel. I hit it hard, and then I hit it again and didn't stop until it stopped moving. When it finally lay still, I left it there like a broken belt on the floor. I thought I'd done Sargent's a favour. Rats are worse than snakes, but who wants a bloody snake loose in a food factory? But when the foreman came in the next morning, he looked like I'd killed his dog. "That was the factory snake," he yelled. "It kept the place clear of rats." It was a pet, more or less. A carpet snake, a diamond python. It didn't bite and didn't bother anyone. They'd had it for years. I was out the door by lunch. I didn't wait to be fired. I thought about that snake for a long time after. The way it looked at me before I hit it. I should have asked first.

They didn't thank me and didn't ask why. They just told me to go even as I was leaving. I never saw the inside of Sargent's again. But I slept better that night knowing I'd killed the damn thing. Pet or not, a man shouldn't have to share his shift with a snake. That's what I told myself then. Now I'm not so sure.

We were six people in one room in Woolloomooloo— four kids, my wife, and me. Paul, Manolete, Cristina and Teresa. I needed to save. I thought maybe one day we'd get a place of our own. The best way to save was to go back to sea. Australian coastal ships paid well, but getting on one wasn't easy. I tried anyway. During the day I waited at the pick-up centre where they selected seamen for the coastal ships. I stayed there until eleven every morning. The union delegate ran the show. He never looked at me when I raised my hand. He'd walk right past me like I was invisible. Day after day, he picked others. I kept showing up. I told myself it was better to die with honour than give up. After three months, he got sick of seeing my face. One morning he called my name. You, for the Iron Duke, he said. I didn't believe it at first.

Us recruits were told to go to the maritime office to sign the contract. Then they told me my seaman's papers weren't good enough. To work Australian coastal ships, you had to spend five years on one ship. I'd never done that. I had fourteen years' experience, but always on the move. That didn't count. I couldn't afford to lose the job. I ran to see Hector Maria Gonzalez López at the Spanish Consulate. He was someone I met along with the other Latinos in the Spanish café in Liverpool Street. I explained the situation but he said it was out of his hands. We sat in silence. Then he excused himself to go to the bathroom. As he left the room, I saw the typewriter. I went to it and typed quickly, all in capital letters:

THIS IS TO CERTIFY ALFONSO MORA SERVED AS AN ABLE SEAMAN ON THE S/S SAN ANTONIO FOR SIX YEARS.

It was a lie. But I needed that job. I found Hector's seal on his desk and stamped the paper with it. When he came back, he saw what I'd done. He didn't say anything. He just looked at me and looked at the paper. Then he signed it. I took it to the maritime office and when they saw that seal, they didn't ask questions. They signed me on as an able seaman. I was a sailor again after a long time on land. I told myself I'd earned it. Fourteen years at sea should count for something. But I knew what I'd done.

Working the coastal ships was good. The union had fought for proper wages and decent conditions. Better than the Americans. But there was a problem. Every time I shipped out, the wife got sick. Her asthma flared up when I was gone. I'd be at sea and think about her struggling to breathe in that one room with four kids. That's when I'd remember the other ones. My kids in England. Three of them, grown now, or nearly grown. I'd left them behind when I left their mother. The sea was always good for wages, good for feeding a family. But you had to leave to earn it. You couldn't be there and be at sea. I'd made that choice twice now. Maybe I was good at leaving. Maybe that's what sailors do. We go away and we come back, and we go away again. But sometimes we don't come back.

I hadn't heard from my kids in England for years. Their mother divorced me, and that was the end of it. I'd remarried and started a new family in Australia. For years there'd been no contact. I hadn't written to my own parents in Spain for fifteen years either. It was Jean who pushed me to write to them. She said it wasn't right, cutting off your own parents. I didn't know what to say to them after all that time, but I wrote and they wrote back. Then one day I came home from a voyage and found a letter waiting. It was from my daughter, Gloria. She had written to my parents, and they gave her my address. We started writing to each other, but the boys never wrote. I didn't blame them. I'd been gone from their lives longer than I'd been in them. But at sea, things were different. On the ships, I found something I hadn't had before. Brothers.

On the coast, I made good mates and somehow became popular. It happened like this. I was working the Port Kembla–Tasmania run on a ship called the Talune. There was an English Australian seaman on board, and we shared what little we had and got on well. I was on the eight-to-twelve watch. One night we left Port Kembla, and after my shift I went to bed. My mate was on the same watch. We were both broke and worried we wouldn't have money for a drink in Hobart. I told him, Don't worry, mate, tomorrow God will provide. I said it like I believed it. He laughed and I laughed. Then I went to sleep.

In the morning, I came up on deck and froze. The ship was torn to bits. The lifeboats were gone, the mainmast had snapped, and the deck was scattered with cargo. I grabbed a fellow seaman and asked what happened. "Big storm", he said. "Hit us hard last night." I hadn't felt a thing. Once I close my eyes, I'm gone. During the war, one of my captains told me I should sleep in the lifeboat. "If we go down, you'll sleep through it," he'd say.

When docked in Hobart the crew stood around on deck looking at the damage and talking about the storm. Someone said the newspapers paid for stories like this. Ten pounds for a good tip. My mate and I looked at each other. We were broke and we had a wrecked ship. So, I went to The Mercury newspaper and told them we'd been hit by a big storm and that the bosun had saved the deck boy from going overboard. It was a lie, but I needed a story. They bit. Two reporters jumped into a car with me, and we drove to the ship. The bosun was working on deck. "Which one is the bosun?" they asked. "Him," I said, pointing.

They snapped his picture and that evening, the front page ran the photo:

THE BOSUN OF THE S. S. TALUNE SAVES DECK BOY FROM SEA.

I made him a hero, and I got my ten pounds. After that, seamen all over the coast wanted to sign on with me. They said I was good luck. I also started making money another way. I'd buy cases of apples in Hobart for seven shillings each and sell them in Sydney for five pounds a case. My cabin smelled like cider. Even the deck was stacked with boxes. One day, the captain walked past and muttered, "Looks like we're running this ship for you." It was good money, but I couldn't stay long. Two trips at most, then I'd have to sign off because the wife was always sick. I had to be there for her and the kids. She'd managed to save a bit and we used it as a deposit on a Housing Commission place out in Seven Hills. As I soon learned, it should've been called Seven Hells. One day, I got back to Sydney from Port Kembla and found Jean gasping for air. Another asthma attack. I stood there and watched her fight for breath, and I knew I couldn't go back to sea. The good money didn't matter. The mates didn't matter. I left the coastal ships and that was the end of my seafaring days.

16

SEVEN HILLS AND A RABBIT CHASE

Australia was a haven for the cunning. It remains one. Had I done in England what I did here, I'd be rich. In Australia, the more crooked you are, the more they seem to appreciate you. Crime is a thriving industry here. Without criminals, there'd be no need for lawyers, judges, or prosecutors. And the politicians? Most are from the legal profession themselves.

I fit in well enough. A man arriving with nothing learns to make his way, and I learned the angles the way other men learn trades. You tell a story when a story opens doors. You bend the truth when the truth keeps you hungry. You take the job that's offered, even when you don't know how to do it, and you figure it out before they notice. In Spain, we called this cleverness. Here, they call it being Australian. A country built by convicts and immigrants understands that survival comes before honesty, and prosperity comes from knowing which rules matter and which ones don't.

The early convicts, mostly from Scotland, England, and Ireland, found themselves without means to return home after serving their sentences. They had no option but to stay and lay the foundations of the nation. Politically, Australia reminded me of pre-civil war Spain, where the king travelled in lavish style while the people suffered in poverty. The leader spent well and the people went without. Much like the Prime Minister of Australia who seemed to spend more time in England than in his own country.

I remembered Spain before the war—men waiting for work that never came, and women stretching meals that couldn't stretch. Leaders spoke of progress while families went hungry. Here it was the same. Men at the top lived well and men at the bottom built the country. I had left one place and found another just like it, but at least here a man could work if he knew how to make himself useful. That was something.

The house on Johnson Avenue, Seven Hills seemed spacious and it came with a large garden. It was different from our room on the bottom floor of the tiny Crown Street terrace in the Loo. It seemed grand, but it was lonely. Too quiet. I'd always lived in cities—crowded, noisy places where you heard voices through the walls and footsteps on the stairs. Now it looked like we were in the bush. Only God knew for how long.

Work was worse out there. In the city, jobs were hard to find. In the bush, they were almost impossible. I got hired once as a painter. It lasted one hour. The boss saw the way I held the brush and said, "That's enough." Painting a ship wasn't the same as painting a house. I knew that after he fired me. Then I tried carpentry. Same result. They could tell I was bluffing. I had been good with my hands once, on the ships, but those skills didn't translate here. A man who knew how to repair an engine in the middle of the ocean was useless when it came to framing a wall. I took these jobs out of necessity, to feed my family and keep up with the bills. Pride had nothing to do with it.

My wife was the real manager in our family. Thanks to her, we scraped by. If it had been up to me, we might have ended up in debtors' prison long ago. She could stretch every dollar, never asking for more than what was given, and she proved herself far better at it than I ever was. I may have underestimated her, or perhaps I had never really looked. On the ships, I had been competent, even skilled. At home, I might have been something less. Meanwhile, I contributed the only way I seemed able. We had three more children—Linda, René and Michelle—in that fresh bush air, bringing our family count to nine. More mouths to feed when I couldn't keep a job for more than an hour. She never did say that much about that. She just made it work.

Malcolm Fraser, a wealthy Australian Prime Minister, once said, "Life was not meant to be easy." He said it to defend his policies when people complained they were making life hard for workers and families. Easy for him to say. I learned the truth of it anyway, whether he meant it the way I understood it or not. All our neighbours were Australians who helped me survive hard times. One got me a job as a boilermaker welder. The work was good and the pay was decent, but it meant three hours of travel each day for twelve-hour shifts, six days a week. Sundays were for yard work and house repairs. It was my property, after all.

I owned land now. That meant something in Australia, even if I was too tired to enjoy it. A man worked to own things and then worked to keep them, and in between there was no time left to understand why he wanted them in the first place. But the work was steady and steady work was rare, so I didn't complain.

My next-door neighbour, Bill Cork, well-connected through his regular pub visits, helped me land a job. He got me work when I needed it most. It would have been good to join him for a drink if only I drank. He drank too much. I heard him through the walls some nights, shouting at his wife. But he helped me when he didn't have to, so what could I say about the rest. A man could be kind to his neighbour and cruel to his wife and still be the reason you fed your family. You learned not to judge too much in Seven Hills.

Sundays, I'd sometimes watch cars pass by, hoping someone would stop. No one ever did. The road went somewhere but not to us. I thought about the early settlers and immigrants then, the ones who built this country. They must have felt this same emptiness, this same waiting. I understood their loneliness better than I understood their courage. Maybe they weren't brave. Maybe they were just stuck like me.

The city job Bill got me was good, but after a year, we were all let go when the firm failed. It happened to good employers. Once again, jobless for three months and behind on payments. Jean grew worried about losing our home and her asthma came back under the stress. Meanwhile, I missed Spain terribly, in a way I'd never felt in the city. It was worse out there in the bush. Bad luck followed me. The days were hard. Spanish music brought tears, and I didn't seem to be much help to my wife.

I thought about ending it. Maybe bad luck wasn't following me. Maybe I made bad choices and called it luck when things went wrong. I didn't know which was true and that made it worse. But I loved my wife and children too much; I just couldn't do that to them. There were nine people who needed feeding and a man doesn't walk away from that. I pushed on.

The children were growing up fast. Paul, the eldest, was a talented soccer player. He went to Spain to develop that talent and he loved it there. But came back to Australia after three years and I never learned why. Maybe Spain wasn't what he hoped for, or maybe what I remembered wasn't real. Manolete learned trumpet with the Seven Hills Brass Band and later made a band with several mates and they toured Australia. He taught himself guitar without costing me a cent and later went to the Sydney Conservatorium, then graduated from Monash University in Melbourne. God helped in ways I didn't expect. My children succeeded where I failed.

Jobless for three months, I heard Riverstone Meatworks needed casual workers. I showed up at five-thirty each morning, but the boss didn't pick me. A week passed like that so I found out his name and had my son write him a letter:

Dear Mr. Percy Fotheringham,
I would appreciate any job for this friend of mine. He's a reliable worker.
Sincerely, Pat Russell.

Each day, I'd come home with rabbit pieces tucked into my riding pants and share them with neighbours. One day I rode back stuffed with rabbits in every pocket of my overalls. Near the end of Vardys Road, the local dogs smelled the rabbits. There were five or six of them and they all had the same idea. I pedalled faster. They ran faster. Dogs were barking and I was pedalling and people started coming out of their houses to see what the noise was about. It seemed like everyone in the neighbourhood was standing on their front steps watching. No one offered help. I made it to my front yard with the pack right behind me, rabbits still in my pockets, and turned the garden hose on them. The neighbours thought it was the best thing they'd seen all week.

In Seven Hills in those early days, entertainment was hard to come by.

The job lasted six months before the plant closed. I found work as a boilermaker soon after, at the same place my neighbour, Bill, worked, half an hour by train from home. After leaving the station, we had to walk miles to work, deep in the middle of nowhere. In the factory, everyone drove except for me and Bill. We had kids instead of cars. After a week of walking, I told Bill, "From now on, we're getting a car every day."

That's when I noticed the Russian. At the factory, there was a Russian migrant who had never owned a car before. But now he had one and acted like he was better than everyone else. He looked down on me and Bill because we didn't have cars. I walked up to him one day and started talking. We talked about this and that. Then we got to boats. Something came out of my mouth that wasn't exactly true. "I have a sixteen-foot boat," I said. "Every weekend we're out fishing at sea." I'd spent years on real ships, working cargo vessels across oceans. Now I was inventing a pleasure boat I'd never seen. The only vessel I captained now was a dinner table with nine mouths to feed.

He asked Bill about it. Bill said, "Oh, yes, he has a beautiful twenty-one footer and sometimes I go out with him." By the end of the day, the boat got bigger still and word had spread around the factory. The Russian was suddenly friendly. The next morning, he offered us a ride to work. Then the morning after that. He ended up driving us every day. Seems he wanted to get to the boat. He asked when we could go out. I told him the engine needed work. Then the weather was bad. Then my wife was sick and I needed to stay home. Then something else. There was always something. I talked about my boat so much that I started to believe it myself. I could see it in my head—white hull, clean deck, the smell of salt water. I'd never been on such a boat. This went on for months.

The factory shut down and once more, I was without work. The labour market in Australia was picking up. Within two weeks, I landed a job close to home, just a ten-minute walk away, as a boilermaker at Carrier Air Conditioning. At the factory, it took two men to assemble one large unit. One day, I walked up to the foreman. "I'll build one of these units each day for you," I said, "but only under one condition."

"And what is that?" he asked.

"You keep your distance and give me all the tools and machinery I need. With that, I'll handle one unit a day."

Everyone was happy with the arrangement. But I lost quite a bit of my wages due to strikes. As I saw it, some union boss higher up was using the movement for personal gain.

At one meeting, I pointed to him on the TV and said, "That man will be Prime Minister of Australia someday."

I wasn't wrong. Bob Hawke governed the country as the 23rd Prime Minister from 1983 till 1991. But being right didn't put money back in my pocket. It didn't change anything for me and my family. Without the trade union, workers in Australia would be as badly off as Blacks in South Africa. In some places they have revolutions. Here we have unions. But it's wrong to use the union for yourself.

At a meeting, I stood up and said my piece. "If we strike, we hold out until our demands are met," I said. "We aren't switches. Turned off and on for someone else's benefit. The union serves the workers, not a few men with ambitions."

Someone told me I was out of order.

I stood. "If I can't speak, I'm leaving."

I walked out. Three hundred men stayed in that hall.

17

A FAMILY DIVIDED BY OCEANS

We had six children when my wife became pregnant with the seventh, a girl, making it four girls and three boys in our family. My wife's father was living with his daughter and her Italian husband and never visited us. When he fell seriously ill, they placed him in an old men's home in Lidcombe, and we went to see him. The building smelled of antiseptic and boiled vegetables. We asked at the desk where to find him then doctor stopped me in the corridor.

"He has a home. Why is he here?" he said.

I felt my jaw tighten. "'He's my wife's father. His daughter—her sister— and her husband dumped him here.'"

The doctor's expression changed. He nodded once and turned. "This way," he said, and led us down a hallway that smelled of disinfectant and boiled vegetables. We found Jean's father slumped in a wheelchair by a grimy window, chin on his chest, alone. He looked smaller than I remembered. No one had shaved him properly. My wife

stood very still when she saw him. She was heavily pregnant
and put one hand on her belly. Then she went to him and
touched his shoulder. I thought of the Queensland trip, years
back, when he'd refused us the money. How certain I'd been
then that I'd never forgive him. But seeing him like that,
forgotten in a corner, the old resentment seemed small and
far away. I told the doctor, "I'm taking him home with me."
Jean said nothing in the taxi ride home, but I saw her wipe
her eyes once. I didn't know if she was grateful or ashamed
that I'd had to be the one to bring him home.

"He'll stay with us," I told her.

She nodded.

The old man lived in the front room. We fed him and
helped him to the bathroom. Sometimes he could walk with
help. Other times he couldn't. In the evenings, when I sat
with him, he would look at me and his eyes would fill. He
never said much, but once he took my hand and held it.

"You're a good man," he said.

I thought about the money he'd refused us all those years
ago. It didn't seem to matter anymore. He stayed with us
through the winter. We did what we could, but the cancer
was winning. When he could no longer eat, we took him back
to the hospital. He died there three days later. Jean went to
see him the day before and when she came home, she was
very quiet.

"He asked about you," she said. "He said to thank you."

We buried him at Rookwood. It rained that day, and there
weren't many people at the grave.

With Bev Cork, our neighbour, watching the children on
weekends, Jean and I began going to the new Spanish Club
in Liverpool Street. We had no car, so we always watched the
clock to catch the last train home at midnight. After a while,
the rush tired us and we stopped going. Then an R.S.L. club
opened in Blacktown, close to home, so I went to join. The

man at the desk looked at my application. "Returned soldiers only," he said.

"I served with the Free French," I told him. "And the Merchant Navy," I shot back.

"Not the same thing."

I leaned forward. "Without the Merchant Navy," I said, "your returned soldiers wouldn't have returned."

He stared at me. A week later, they sent a letter inviting me to join.

I went back. The club was full of Germans and Italians, men who'd fought for the other side. They sat drinking beer, laughing, members in good standing. I stood at the bar and finished one drink. Then I left and never went back.

Years passed. My first wife, Dorothy, remarried an American, and they moved to the States with my children. My daughter, Gloria, wrote to me, and I wrote back. I was careful with my words, formal, treating her as I would an adult I respected. I did not know what else to do. The letters came regularly, and I kept them in a draw in our bedroom. Jean never said much about them, but I knew she noticed. At dinner, sometimes, there would be silence. Not the comfortable kind.

One evening she put down her fork. "You need to go see them."

"Who?"

"Don't do that," she said. "You know who."

"We can't afford it."

"That's not why you won't go."

I looked at her. "Then why?"

"I don't know," she said. "But they're always here in this house. And I'm sick of living with ghosts."

"How would I even get there?"

"We could save."

"On what I earn?"

She stood up and started clearing the plates. "Then keep sending your money orders. Keep playing your pools. But go. Get it out of your system."

The conversation ended there. Good jobs were hard to come by and I had one nearby. I wasn't about to quit and start over somewhere else. But she was right about one thing—I couldn't stop thinking about them. Every week I sent money orders to England. Small amounts, but regular. I played the Pools on Saturdays, checking the results in the newspaper on Sunday mornings. A big win would pay for the airfare. Years went by like this—the letters, the money orders, the pools. Then one Saturday, when I checked the results, it seemed my luck might finally have turned. Whether it had turned enough, I would have to see.

But winning, I thought, would probably change nothing. If anything, it might make things worse. Now that a trip was possible, I kept thinking about Spain even more than ever. Not the war—Spain before all that. My mother's face. My sisters. The street where I grew up. I'd left them behind twenty years ago, and for what? At night I lay awake thinking about my mother, wondering if she thought about me.

Jean noticed. The children especially notice. It seemed that they too longed for Spain even though they only knew it from my memories. After all it's mostly all I could ever talk about. I could feel the strain I was putting on everyone. Spain had happened a lifetime ago, but it lived in our house, making everyone uncomfortable. It was a strange, intense yearning— not quite grief, not quite homesickness. Something deeper. I think it made them all feel like their lives were incomplete, like they were living someone else's story. Once I found one of my sons sitting alone in his room, staring at nothing. When I asked what was wrong, he said quietly, 'I want to go to Spain.' He'd never been there. He was ten years old. I knew I was wearing them all down, but I couldn't shake it.

That was when I knew how deep the damage went. And then a letter arrived from my daughter, Gloria, in America. One of my sons, Ricardo, had joined the American Army. They were sending him to Vietnam. I read the letter and sat very still. Australia would soon be sending soldiers too. I thought about Ricardo going to war in a place he'd never been, leaving his family. Just like I had. I lay awake at night thinking that maybe he needed me, that maybe after all these years it was time to make amends. I even thought about joining the Australian Merchant Navy again, getting to Vietnam somehow. Ridiculous. By then I was too old. The war would be fought without me, and my son would go alone, the way young men always do.

But what did I know about Ricardo anymore? When he was a boy in England, I'd wanted him to be a bullfighter. His mother had laughed at that. She wanted him to be a doctor. Now he was in Vietnam with the medical corps. He'd listened to her, not me. Later I learned he went to university in the States and became one of the top dermatologists in America. He never wrote to me. I can only guess at his reasons, though I think he may be wrong about them.

My oldest son, Rafael, in Pennsylvania did well too. He was General Manager of a factory and married now. He didn't write either. But one of his daughters did. She wanted to meet me. That was when I started thinking seriously about the trip. Not just to see Ricardo or make peace with the past, but because someone actually wanted to see me. After all these years, how could I simply show up and say, 'I am your father'?

The children from my second marriage—my marriage to Jean—were grown now too. They'd started their own families in Australia. The two eldest boys, Paul and Manolete, had started their own families. My eldest daughter, Cristina, married an Italian, a kind man. It was hard at first as I couldn't help thinking about Italians and the Spanish Civil War, what they'd done. But he was good to her, so I let it go. The second daughter, Teresa, also married an Italian. In both the Spanish Civil War and the Second World War, the Italians were the enemy. Now I had two of them at my dinner table.

Thinking about family brought Spain back. It had been thirty-four years since I'd last seen my family in Spain. My youngest sister, Carmen, had been just a baby when I left— now I heard she'd married a Spanish millionaire, Pepe, and was doing well. When one of my daughters was getting married, I decided to invite them. I sent the invitation not knowing what to expect. The telegram came back: they would come. I thought about seeing Carmen again after all those years. The last time I'd held her, she was an infant. Now she had two daughters of her own. I waited for the wedding day.

We went to Mascot airport. I stood at the gate watching the sky for their plane. When I saw it coming in to land, my eyes filled. I couldn't help it. We waited at the arrivals gate. The flight landed but they didn't come through. I asked at the desk and they said they'd missed their connection in Rome. All that waiting, all those tears at seeing the plane, for nothing. But they arrived the next day. Carmen came through first, and I hardly recognized her. We embraced without speaking. Then her husband, Pepe, her two daughters and my mother came through. We took them home to Seven Hills.

For two days, everything was good. We talked, ate together, showed them the house, the neighbourhood. Then on the third morning, my mother asked, "What time does the plane for Madrid leave?" I stared at her. "Why the hell did you come here if you want to go back so quickly?" The words came out harder than I meant. She looked away. After thirty-four years apart, she was already thinking about leaving.

My brother-in-law, Pepe, turned out to be a decent man. The millionaire part was true—he owned property in Madrid and spoke about his jewellery store business with the easy confidence of someone who'd made money. We sat on the back porch in the evenings, and he talked about Spain. How much it had changed since I'd left. New buildings, new government, different people in charge.

One night he said, "If you come back to Spain, I'll set you up. One of my flats. Help you start a business." I looked at him. "Why would you do that?"

"You're family," he said. He shrugged. "And my wife misses you. Your mother misses you. They want you closer."

I didn't know what to say. I'd been gone thirty-four years and now this man I barely knew was offering to bring me home. After that, my mother's question about the Madrid flight made more sense. She wasn't leaving—she was already planning my return.

After they left, I went back to work. Same factory, same shifts, same routine. I read the newspaper in the mornings— mostly ads for department stores. Sometimes there was news about Vietnam or politics, but it felt distant, like it was happening to someone else. We had a television now. At night we'd sit and watch it, but there wasn't much worth watching. The work was steady, and I should have been grateful. But I'd grown to hate it. Getting up at the same time every morning, going to the same place, coming home tired. Jean could tell.

"You're not happy," she said one evening.

"I'm fine."

"No," she said. "You're not."

She was right. We used to go dancing on weekends, go into the city when we had money. But the girls were in private school now—uniforms, books, fees. The expenses kept growing so we stayed home.

One night I said to her, "Remember what Pepe offered? The flat in Spain. The business."

She looked at me for a long time. "You serious."

"I don't know," I said. "Maybe."

But I did know. After they'd left, after seeing my mother and sister again, something had shifted. Australia felt temporary, like I was still just passing through.

Money was tight and Jean took a job as a nurse aide at the local hospital. She worked the early shift, leaving before dawn and taking two buses to get there. A month later, the phone rang at work. She'd been in an accident on her way home. The bus had collided with a truck. She was all right—bruised, shaken—but all right. That night I sat with her. She had a bandage on her forehead and moved carefully, like everything hurt.

"You can't keep doing this," I said.

"We need the money."

"Not like this."

Then a letter came from Spain. My father had died. The news was weeks old by the time it reached me. I'd never see him again, never have the chance to explain why I'd left, why I'd stayed away. My mother was alone now. As I sat at the kitchen table with the letter in my hand Jean came and stood behind me, her hand on my shoulder.

"We should go," I said.

"To Spain?"

"Pepe offered me a flat and help starting a business. We could use the money from selling this house and start over."

I waited for her to say no, to list all the reasons it was impossible. Instead, she was quiet for a long time.

"All right," she said finally. "Let's sell."

I looked at her. "You're sure?"

"You've been searching for something," she said. "Maybe it's there."

Three weeks later, we sold the house. Eighteen years in Seven Hills, and it was gone in an afternoon. We signed the papers and took the check. We organized passports, bought tickets on the Italian liner Galileo Galilei. Four of us would go—Jean, myself, our two youngest daughters, Linda and Michelle, and our youngest son, René. The older children, Paul, Manolete, Cristina and Teresa would stay in Sydney. They had their own lives now.

Jean had rarely been out of Sydney let alone Australia. This would be her first time on a ship, her first time crossing an ocean. She was doing it for me. We went shopping for new clothes—dresses for her, a suit for me. She picked out an evening gown. "We should dress for dinner on the ship," she said. "Make it special."

"Like a honeymoon," I said.

She smiled. "A second one."

The morning we left, the family came to the wharf to see us off. Cristina and Teresa stood with their husbands and children. Manolete lived in Bathurst now, too far to come. Paul lived on the outskirts of Sydney. Neither could make it. The ship's horn sounded, and the crew cast off the mooring lines. I stood at the rail watching them. Cristina was crying. Teresa had her arm around her. The grandchildren waved, not understanding what was happening. Only two of my daughters there to say goodbye.

As Sydney Harbor opened up behind us, something turned in my chest. I thought about Manolete and Paul, not there because they lived too far away. And Cristina and Teresa, crying on the dock. And my children from England I hadn't seen in years. And Ricardo in Vietnam. Always distance. Always separation. What had I done? I was leaving them the same way I'd left my children in England, the same way I'd left Spain. Always leaving. I gripped the rail. For a moment, I wanted to jump, to swim back to shore, to undo it all. But the ship kept moving. The figures on the dock became dots, then nothing. We were bound for Spain.

By late afternoon, there was nothing but ocean. I stood on the deck watching the wake trail behind us, white foam disappearing into grey water. Jean had gone below to unpack, arranging our things in the small cabin we'd have for the next six weeks. But the evening gown stayed in the suitcase. So did my suit. The Galileo Galilei was nothing like I'd imagined. No grand dining room with white tablecloths. No passengers in evening dress. Just narrow corridors and cramped cabins that smelled of diesel and sweat.

The Australians boarded in thongs and shorts, some even carrying plastic bags instead of luggage. They looked like they were heading to the beach, not to Europe. Jean and I stood on the deck in our traveling clothes, overdressed and out of place. The first night, I went to the cabin to change for dinner. Jean looked at me putting on the suit.

"Don't," she said.

"Why not?"

"Just don't."

She was right. In the dining room, everyone wore the same clothes they'd boarded in. We sat at a long table with families from New Zealand heading to Fiji. Children running everywhere. People shouting over each other. It felt more like a refugee ship than an ocean liner.

The second day out, a fight broke out on the deck. Two men, drunk, swinging at each other while their wives screamed. The crew broke it up eventually, but after that, Jean stayed in the cabin most of the time.

"This isn't what you promised," she said.

She was right about that too. I'd sold her on a dream—a romantic voyage, a second honeymoon, a new life in Spain. But here we were, stuck on a boat full of strangers in thongs, the diesel smell making her sick, nothing romantic about any of it.

Three days out, the sea turned rough. The ship began to pitch and roll. Water came over the bow, washing across the deck. I held onto the rail and watched the horizon disappear, then reappear, then disappear again. Jean stayed in the cabin, sick. The children too. I brought them water and crackers, but they couldn't keep anything down. The cabin smelled of vomit and sweat.

By the second night, the storm was worse. The ship rolled hard to one side, held there for a moment, then rolled back the other way. Things slid off tables. A chair tipped over in the corridor. Jean gripped the edge of the bunk, her face white. I could hear children crying in the next cabin. I stood in the doorway, bracing myself against the frame.

"Are we going to die?" Jean asked.

"No."

"You don't know that."

She was right. I didn't know that. The ship groaned and creaked. I thought about the children. I thought about drowning in the middle of the ocean, all of us together, all because I'd wanted to go back to Spain.

"It's just a storm," I said. "It'll pass."

It did pass. By the third morning, the sea was calmer. Later I heard we'd narrowly missed a cyclone. A few hours' difference and we would have been in the centre of it. When we reached Fiji, Jean was the first one off the ship. She stood on the dock and looked back at the Galileo Galilei.

"I'm not getting back on," she said.

"We have to."

"I don't care. Find another way."

But there was no other way. We walked into town. The children ran ahead on the street, happy to be on solid ground. Michelle came up to me and said, "I need money to buy something."

"How much?"

"You owe me five dollars. From the wharf."

I'd forgotten completely. Before we'd left Australia, I'd been out of change, and she'd lent me five dollars. I pulled out my wallet and gave her seven thousand liras.

"That's a lot," she said.

"It's the same as five dollars," I told her.

She went into a shop while Jean and I walked along the harbor and had lunch at a restaurant. For a while, she seemed better. The sun was warm. She held my arm.

"It's beautiful here," she said. "We could stay."

I didn't answer.

Michelle came back holding a small scarf.

"This cost seven thousand liras," she said. She wasn't smiling.

"The exchange rate—" I started.

"I know," she said, and walked away.

That evening, we walked back to the ship. Jean stopped at the gangway and stood looking up at it.

"I can't," she said.

"I know."

She took a breath and started up. I followed her back to the diesel smell, the narrow cabin, the rough sea ahead.

From Fiji to Tahiti, the weather stayed rough. Then from Tahiti to Acapulco, it got worse. Jean spent most of her time lying down. She couldn't eat. Couldn't keep water down. Her skin turned grey.

"You need to see the doctor," I said.

I took her to the ship's hospital. The doctor examined her, gave her some pills, told her to rest. She stayed there two days.

Tahiti was different. Warm air, palm trees, clear water. We had twenty-four hours on land. Jean smiled for the first time since we'd left Australia. The children swam. We ate fresh fruit and walked on the beach. For a day, we forgot about the ship.

Then we had to go back.

From Tahiti to Acapulco, Jean got worse. I took her to the ship's hospital. The doctor examined her, gave her some pills, told her to rest. She stayed there two days. I visited in the mornings and evenings, sitting on a metal chair beside the narrow bed.

When we reached Acapulco, the harbor was too shallow for the ship. We anchored offshore. A motorboat came out to ferry passengers to land. It was crowded—maybe forty people, luggage piled in the middle, children sitting on their parents' laps. The sea was choppy. The motorboat rose and fell, smacking hard against the waves. Water came over the side, soaking everyone. One woman started screaming. Her husband tried to calm her, but she wouldn't stop. The children began crying. I held onto the side of the boat with one hand and Jean with the other. She was grey, weak from being sick. Our daughters clutched the seats, eyes wide.

"We're going to sink," Jean said.

"We're not going to sink."

"Look at the water."

There was water in the bottom of the boat now, sloshing around our feet. The engine sputtered, caught again, sputtered. I thought about drowning in Acapulco harbor after surviving the storm at sea. After selling the house, leaving the children, enduring six weeks on that ship. Drowning in a motorboat fifty yards from shore. The engine held. We made it to the dock. Everyone climbed out, soaked, shaking. Jean sat on a bench and put her head in her hands.

"I can't do this anymore," she said.

I sat beside her. "I know."

"We still have to get to Spain."

"I know."

She looked at me. "Was it worth it?"

I didn't answer. I couldn't.

Later, when I thought about it, it seemed almost funny. All those people crammed in that boat, screaming, certain we were going to die. But at the time, there was nothing funny about it. We had a full day in Acapulco. The children went off on their own to explore. Jean and I walked through the town. Music came from somewhere. I stopped.

"What is it?" Jean asked.

"Listen."

It was Mexican music. Mariachi. The sound of trumpets and guitars carrying through the street. I'd played this music on my gramophone at Seven Hills, scratchy records I'd bought years ago. But this was live. This was real. We followed the music to a courtyard where a wedding was happening. People everywhere, bright colours, a band playing right there in front of us. Someone waved us in. We were strangers, but it didn't matter. They gave us drinks and food. Everyone was dancing.

I stood watching the band. The trumpet player caught my eye and nodded, kept playing. The music I'd listened to alone in Seven Hills, trying to remember Mexico, trying to hold onto something from my travels. And here it was, all around me.

Jean leaned close. "This is what I imagined," she said. "Not the ship. This."

"I know."

We stayed for hours. The music, the dancing, the warmth—it felt like being alive again after all those weeks at sea.

Later, we passed by a telephone exchange and I stood looking at it for a while.

"Call her," Jean said.

"Who?"

"You know who. We're close now. Call Gloria."

I'd left her in England when she was eight years old. She was a woman now, living in America. I hadn't spoken to her in years. I didn't know if she'd even want to talk to me. But I went into the shop and gave the operator the number. The phone rang. Once. Twice. Then her voice.

"Hello?"

"It's your father."

Silence. Then: "Papa?"

I hadn't heard that word in so long. Papa. My throat tightened.

"I'm in Acapulco," I said. "On my way to Spain."

"You're so close."

"I know."

"I thought—" She stopped. "I didn't think you'd call."

"I should have called years ago."

"Yes." Her voice broke. "You should have."

We talked for twenty minutes. She told me about her life, her husband, her work. I told her about the ship, about going back to Spain. She said she wanted to see me. I said I'd come visit, that we weren't far anymore, that I'd make it right.

When I hung up, Jean was waiting outside.

"How was it?" she asked.

"Good," I said. "It was good."

But I felt hollow. Twenty minutes on the phone after all those years apart. She'd called me "Papa." My children with Jean called me "Dardy"—their own odd word for it. Two different families, two different names. Papa and Dardy. Neither one quite felt like me.

That night, back on the ship, I lay awake thinking about her voice saying "Papa." Thinking about all the years she'd waited for me to call, to write, to come back. And now I was on my way to Spain, moving away again.

From Acapulco, we sailed to Panama. We had a few hours on land before the ship left again. Jean wanted to walk, to see the city and the children came along. We wandered through narrow streets, passing old buildings, washing hanging from balconies, and there was the spicy smell of food cooking. Nobody else from the ship around. Just us, walking deeper into the city without thinking about where we were going.

A police officer appeared at the end of an alley. He waved at us, so we walked toward him.

"Don't go that way," he said in Spanish.

"Why not?"

"Two people killed there last night."

I looked down the street. It looked the same as the street we'd just walked.

"We came from there," I said.

He stared at me. "You're lucky."

We walked back. Jean was quiet. Later, on the ship, she said, "We should be more careful."

"Yes."

She turned over in the bunk.

From Panama, we sailed for Lisbon. Seven days crossing the Atlantic. I'd crossed it many times during the war, knew how rough it could be. But I said nothing to Jean.

The crossing was calm. Smooth water, good weather. The ship moved steady. Jean started to come on deck again, to sit in the sun with the children. She looked better. The gray left her face.

"It's nice now," she said one afternoon.

"Yes."

"Why wasn't it like this before?"

I didn't have an answer.

Thirty-one days since we'd left Australia. Seven of them peaceful, finally. At night, I stood at the rail watching the water. After everything - the storm near Fiji, the near-cyclone,

Jean in the hospital, the motorboat in Acapulco, Panama - now the Atlantic was giving us calm.

When we reached Lisbon, Jean cried. Not from sadness. From relief.

We spent the day walking through the city. Old streets, tile buildings, people speaking Portuguese. The children ate pastries. We sat at a cafe. For the first time since leaving Australia, Jean smiled like she meant it.

That night we boarded for Málaga. One more leg. Then Spain.

Just past midnight, I woke to the ship rolling. I got up and looked out the porthole. The sea was rough again. Getting rougher. I went up on deck. The wind had picked up. Rain coming sideways. The ship pitched hard.

A crew member passed. "Storm came up fast," he said. "Captain's taking us out to sea, away from the coast."

I went back to the cabin. Jean was awake.

"Another storm?" she asked.

"Yes."

"Of course there is."

She didn't sound angry. Just tired. Like she'd expected it.

The storm lasted through the night. By morning, we were far off course, out in the open ocean. It took another day to get back and make landfall at Málaga.

18

THEY SHUT ME DOWN

The sea was rough. The weather held us back. When we finally docked in Malaga, I had been gone thirty-five years. We took the bus to Madrid. The fields rolled past the windows. Yellow and empty. No workers in them. I watched the fields and wondered where the people had gone. Pepe met us at the station. He embraced me and kissed my wife.

"The flat is ready," he said.

That night the family came and my sister, Carmen, cooked. The children asked about Australia. We drank wine and talked late. The next day they came again. The third day Pepe came alone. The visits grew shorter after that.

I took Jean through the streets I remembered. The buildings stood unchanged, the same stone and narrow passages, but the city felt wrong. We sat in a café and at the next table two men argued about football - Real Madrid had won, Barcelona would lose the championship. Their voices were flat.

Later that evening I asked Pepe, "Where are the people from before?"

"Franco moved them out. He brought people from Andalusia, Aragon. From Murcia. From everywhere."

"Why?"

"To quiet the city."

The old Madrid had fought Franco for three years. Now the streets were full of people from other provinces—Andalusians, Valencianos, people who had not fought for the city, who did not remember the siege. I walked through the neighbourhoods near our flat. Men stood on corners leaning against walls and smoked. No one was going anywhere. They spoke with different accents. I listened for the Madrid I remembered but didn't hear it. Outside a closed factory, a group of men smoked and talked about last night's match, Real Madrid had scored three goals.

As an Australian citizen, I had to report to the police station every week. The first time I went, I brought my passport and my Spanish birth certificate. The building was grey stone with narrow windows. Two guards stood at the entrance with machine guns, their fingers resting near the triggers.

Inside, I showed the clerk my documents.

"Australian," he said. He did not look at the birth certificate.

"I was born in Barcelona," I said.

"But you are Australian now."

He wrote in a ledger and stamped a paper.

"You will report here every Monday. Ten o'clock."

"For how long?"

"Every Monday," he said again.

The guards watched me leave then I walked back through streets I had known as a boy. The buildings were the same, but the people were not. Their voices sounded wrong. Their concerns were not mine.

That night I told Jean, "Every week I must report, like a criminal."

"But you were born here."

"It does not matter."

I had lost it. Not just the old Madrid, but my right to be Spanish. They had taken it from me twice—once when I left, and again when I returned.

But I was not silent about it. One night we went to a bar near the flat. We sat at a table in the back and ordered wine. The place was full, mostly men drinking and talking. Most of the conversation was about football, the usual talk. Then an explosion echoed from somewhere outside, not close, but loud enough to rattle the glasses. The bar went quiet for a moment. Then the voices started again and Jean gripped my arm. She was not used to this. In Australia there were no bombs.

"It's nothing," I said. But the sound had stirred something in me.

At the next table, two men talked about the explosion. One of them said the word—terrorists. E.T.A.

I could not contain myself and I turned to them.

"Why worry now?" I said. "For three years, bombs fell on this city every night. Nobody spoke up then."

The men looked at me and the bar grew quieter.

"The real terrorists were Franco and his cronies," I said.

Again, the men at the tables looked at me. One started to speak but I kept going.

"The E.T.A. fought as Maquis in the French mountains. Against the Germans. They helped the Allies."

"That was years ago," one of the men said.

"After the war they were dumped," I said. "Now they continue the fight. It's the same war, against Franco."

"They kill people," the other man said.

"Franco killed more."

The bar was very quiet now.

"They're not terrorists," I said. "They're freedom fighters."

Everyone was listening. Jean's hand on my arm became tighter as one of the men at the next table nodded and said, "You're right. But watch yourself. This place has secret police." I had been in Madrid long enough to know the risk. But I had spoken anyway. It felt necessary.

A few days later, Pepe invited us to meet some of his business associates. We went to a different bar, quieter, more expensive. The men were older, well-dressed. They had done well under Franco.

The conversation turned to politics. One of them complained about strikes. Another about the students.

"You're from Australia," one man said to me. "You understand. What they did to your Prime Minister—Whitlam. That's what we needed here a clean removal. No civil war."

I didn't know what he meant. I had left Australia before any news reached me.

"What happened to Whitlam?" I said.

"They dismissed him. The Governor-General. November eleventh." He smiled. "Very civilized."

I felt something cold move through me. Dismissed. I supported Whitlam.

"The Governor-General dismissed him?" I said.

"Yes. Constitutional crisis. The Senate blocked supply. The Governor-General acted. Very proper."

The other men nodded. They thought this proved something.

I said nothing more. These men saw Whitlam's removal as a model for what Franco should have done—remove an elected government without bloodshed. They didn't know I had supported Whitlam. That I believed in what he tried to do.

I finished my drink. My country had removed its Prime Minister while I was in Spain. The man who smiled at me across the table thought this made Australia wise. I thought it made us something else.

My money was running out. I needed work.

I asked Pepe for help. He made some calls. A few days later he came by the flat.

"I found something," he said. "Welding. A factory in the industrial district."

"How did you manage it?"

"I know a man who knows the foreman. It's not much, but it's work."

The factory was an hour away by bus. The building was old brick, windows dark with grime. Inside, the air smelled of metal and oil. The foreman showed me the welding equipment.

"You know how to use this?" he said.

"Yes."

"Good. Start tomorrow. Seven o'clock."

On my first day, I walked onto the factory floor and stopped. "The cables were old. The rubber covering had split in places. I could see the copper wire inside. Electric cables lay scattered across the concrete. They were old, rubber coverings split in places, and I could see the exposed copper wire inside. No warning signs. Men stepped over them as if they weren't there. I called to the man who worked the station next to mine. He was older, maybe late fifties.

"How do you work like this?" I said. I pointed at the wires.

He shrugged. "You get used to it."

"Is there no union? Someone to complain to?"

"There's a union."

"Then why don't they fix this?"

"The boss is the union delegate," he said.

I looked at him. He looked back at me. His face showed nothing.

"The boss?"

"Yes."

I understood then. Unions were meant to protect the workers, but the man who ran the union was the same man who ignored the danger. It was Franco's Spain in miniature—the appearance of protection, the reality of control. I bent over my work. The exposed wires stayed where they were. In Australia, this would have shut down the factory. Here, no one said anything. No one could.

The lunch whistle blew. I set down my tools. I looked around. Everyone else kept working. They didn't stop. They didn't even look up. Even in East Africa, diving underwater to chain logs, the men would stop when the lunch whistle blew. They would surface and rest. Here, no one stopped. They didn't even look up. The next day I arrived at the factory. The foreman met me at the gate.

"You don't need to come in," he said.

"What?"

"Your services are no longer needed."

"I just started yesterday."

"I know."

He turned and walked back inside.

I went to see Pepe that evening. He listened, then picked up the phone. He spoke to someone for a long time. When he hung up, he looked relieved.

"My friend will speak to the boss," he said. "Wait until Friday. He'll fix it."

"Tell your friend to thank the boss for me," I said.

"Good. I'll ...."

"Tell him he can take his factory and shove it."

Pepe stared at me. His face went pale.

"You don't mean that."

"I mean it."

"But the job—"

"I don't want it back."

He said nothing. We sat in silence. I had insulted the man who had helped him. I had refused the favour Pepe had worked to arrange. But I would not work in that factory again.

Weeks passed. I had no work and Pepe had been avoiding me. One morning I went to his house and knocked on the door. He answered but didn't invite me in.

"You promised to set me up in business," I said. "Back in Australia. You promised."

He looked down the street, then back at me.

"Come with me," he said.

We walked to one of his vacant shops. The windows were dirty and inside, the floor was concrete and the walls needed paint.

"You can fix it up," he said. "Open a fruit shop. Get your wife and family working. We'll split the profits."

I looked at the empty shop then looked at him.

"Split the profits?"

"Yes. Fifty-fifty."

"I do the work. My family runs it and you get half."

"I own the building."

"I came all this way for this?"

He said nothing.

"I didn't come to Spain to be exploited," I said.

I walked out and we never spoke again.

My mother lived with my sister and Pepe in a house that was large and comfortable. His money was obvious. My mother had a room of her own, a maid to help her. She visited us once, maybe twice. Our flat was small and hot and she didn't stay long. One afternoon she came by in midsummer, the heat was unbearable. She took the only chair with a fan. 'It's unbearable,' she said. 'How do you live like this?'"

"You have air conditioning at my sister's house," I said.

"Yes, but—"

"Then you have everything there. Why come here to complain?"

"You're my son."

"If there's a God, he should punish you and Pepe both."

She stood up, her face white and left without saying goodbye.

Jean looked at me but said nothing. She knew what I had done. I had insulted my mother and had cut off Pepe. We had nowhere to go now. But I couldn't stop myself. I had never been able to. When I saw something wrong, I said it. It didn't matter who was listening. It didn't matter what it cost. And I would not work for a Spanish boss again. Not after the factory.

I bought a newspaper and looked through the classifieds. A dry fruit shop was for sale. It came with a small truck. I went to see it. The price was reasonable, so I bought it. The business was simple. I bought chips in bulk, thirty barrels a week, and packaged them in smaller bags. I loaded them in the truck and drove to bars and shops around Madrid. The bars paid cash, the shops paid weekly.

The problem was the deliveries. When I left to drive the truck, the shop had to close as Jean couldn't run it. She didn't speak Spanish and the kids were too young. So, I would close the shop, make the deliveries, come back and open again. It worked and the business grew.

Then the telegram came. It was from America. From my daughter—Gloria, my first wife's child. She was coming to Spain and wanted to see me. I read the telegram twice. I hadn't seen her in years. Not since I left England. Her mother had remarried, and I didn't know what Gloria even looked like now let alone what she thought of me. Jean was standing in the doorway of the shop watching me stare at the telegram.

"What is it?" she said.

"My daughter, Gloria, from America. She's coming here."

"When?"

"Two weeks."

She said nothing. We both understood what this meant. The past was coming to our door. I had two weeks. I tried not to think about it. I ran the shop, made my deliveries, packaged the chips into bags. Jean asked me once what Gloria looked like now. I realized I didn't know. She had been eight when I left, now she was twenty-three.

We met her at the airport. I recognized her from her mother—the same hair, the same way of standing. She embraced me and smiled at Jean and the children. Her Spanish was good.

"Thank you for having me," she said to Jean.

"You're welcome," Jean said. "We're glad you're here."

We took her back home. She looked around at the small flat but didn't say anything about it. The first few days went well enough. Jean cooked meals Gloria liked and took her around Madrid. Gloria was polite. She asked about the shop, about our life in Spain. But something was wrong. I noticed it in small things. The way Gloria's smile disappeared when she looked at Jean. The way she spoke to me when Jean wasn't in the room—warm, affectionate—and how she changed when Jean returned. Cool. Distant. One evening, Jean prepared a special dinner. She had spent all afternoon cooking but Gloria just picked at her food.

"Is something wrong?" Jean asked.

"No. I'm just not very hungry."

"You should eat something. You're too thin."

"I'm fine."

Jean looked at me. I said nothing. What could I say?

Later, after Gloria went to bed, Jean sat at the kitchen table.

"She hates me," she said.

"She doesn't hate you."

"You haven't seen it?"

I had seen it. I just didn't want to admit it.

"Her letters were so warm," Jean said. "She said she wanted to meet me. To know her father's new family."

"Maybe she's just adjusting."

"It's been a week."

I had no answer for that.

The tension grew while Gloria's politeness became a weapon. She thanked Jean for everything with a coldness that was worse than rudeness. Jean tried harder—cooking, cleaning, offering to take Gloria places. She accepted everything with the same frozen courtesy.

I tried to talk to Gloria one day when we were alone in the shop.

"Jean is trying," I said.

"I know. She tries very hard."

"Then why—"

"Why what?"

"Why do you treat her like that?"

Gloria looked at me. "Like what?"

"You know what I mean."

"She's very nice," Gloria said. Her voice was flat. "You're lucky to have found someone so nice."

I looked at her and didn't know what to say.

Gloria's resentment didn't fade. It grew worse. Each night she wanted to go out—bars, clubs, late into the morning. I went with her as I thought it would help. It didn't. Jean stopped trying and stayed home with the children. Gloria barely spoke to her.

One night Gloria and I sat in a bar near the shop. It was three in the morning.

"Why did you leave us?" she said.

"It was complicated."

"That's not an answer."

"Your mother and I couldn't stay married."

"So you left."

"Yes."

"And married her."

I didn't know what to say. Everything I said would be wrong.

"She's not why I left," I said.

"I don't believe you."

We sat in silence, in a bar that was almost empty. I had tried to make it right with Gloria, but it couldn't be made right.

A week later I told her she needed to go back to America because of her visa. I said she couldn't stay longer without getting problems. That was the lie I told her. The truth was I couldn't watch Jean suffer anymore. And Gloria knew. She knew exactly why I was sending her away.

"You're choosing her," she said.

"I'm not choosing anyone."

"You just did."

She left the next week barely saying goodbye to Jean. She embraced me at the airport and was crying.

"I wanted us to be a family again," she said.

"We can't go back."

"I know."

That was the last time I saw her.

The shop kept me busy. I worked alone now, packaging chips, making deliveries and the business was good. I had regular customers and was making money. Then the policeman came. He walked into the shop one afternoon, looked around and asked for my work permit.

"I don't have one," I said.

"You need one."

"I'm Spanish. I was born in Barcelona."

He looked at my papers. My Australian passport and my Spanish birth certificate.

"You're Australian now," he said. "You need a work permit."

"How do I get one?"

"You can't. Your visa is for visiting only, not for working."

"But I own this shop."

"That doesn't matter. The law is the law."

He told me I had to close the shop, that I had one week to sell everything and leave. If I didn't, they would arrest me. I went home and told Jean. She sat at the table and didn't say anything at first.

"They're shutting you down," she said finally.

"Yes."

"Because you're not really Spanish."

"That's what they said."

She looked at me. "They did the same thing your brother-in-law did. They let you think you belonged here and then they took it away."

She was right. Spain had rejected me twice now. Once when I had to leave as a boy and now, when I tried to come back as a man. I sold the inventory and sold the truck. I didn't get much. But I had been careful and hadn't put everything into the business and had enough for tickets back to Australia. We left Spain a month later. I thought about going to see Pepe. I thought about telling my mother goodbye. But I did neither. We just left.

On the plane, Jean asked me if I was sad.

"No," I said.

But I was lying. I had tried to go home. There was no home to go to. That much was clear.

I loved Spain. My family loved it too. But I despised the system there. During the war, in England, class distinctions blurred. I was a sailor in the French forces. I wore my uniform to the Seven Seas Club in London. I drank with high-ranking British officers. Once I dated an aristocrat's daughter. Nobody cared about rank when bombs were falling. I worked in an English factory then. It was large— larger than anything in Spain. The boss sometimes worked beside me on the line. Sometimes he borrowed a cigarette from me. We were all workers. That was democracy.

Spain was different. The class structure was rigid. It never changed. Even during the Civil War, you could tell who was who. The divisions stayed. Maybe England has changed since then. I don't know. But working there during the war was good. Everyone was equal because everyone was fighting. Australian capitalists reminded me of the Spanish ones. They rose from working-class backgrounds. From nothing much. That made them harder on workers. They remembered being poor and they hated it. They made sure you remembered it too. But Australia had trade unions. Strong ones. A man could stand up. In Spain, the boss was the union delegate. In Australia, the union fought the boss. That was the difference.

I learned something from all this. Democracy isn't about where you're born. It's about whether you can stand up to the man who has power over you. In England during the war, you could. In Australia, if you had a union, you could. In Franco's Spain, you couldn't.

That's why they shut me down. Not because I didn't have papers. Because I thought I could stand up. Spain changed something in me. I had loved the country. The land, the people, the memory of my childhood. But living under

Franco's system killed that love. What remained was anger at how things worked there. The hierarchy. The arrogance. The silence. In Australia, you could tell your boss to go to hell if he was wrong. You might lose your job, but you could say it. In Spain, you stayed silent or you disappeared.

I couldn't live like that.

I decided to leave. Some might call it defeat. I called it survival. I had learned one thing from history: a man who burns his ships behind him better be sure he can win the battle ahead. Cortez burned his ships in Mexico and conquered an empire. But he had an army. I had a wife, children, and a failing shop in Franco's Madrid.

I kept money aside. Always. From the first day I opened the shop, I put money where they couldn't find it. Not in a bank—banks talked to the government. I kept cash hidden in the flat. Enough for tickets. Enough to start again. When the policeman shut me down, I knew that money had saved us. We could leave. We had a way out.

Some men stay and fight lost battles. I had fought enough of those. This time, I chose to leave while I still could. That wasn't cowardice. That was knowing when you were beaten.

We left Spain for Australia a month later.

19

NO PLACE LIKE HOME, EXCEPT WHEN THERE IS

I tried to sell the business, but no one could buy it. No one had the money. Time was slipping by, and I had to leave. I told my cousin Pili to take it over and sell the business and the truck and send me the proceeds or keep it and pay me whenever you can. Either way was fine with me. But as it turned out, years passed and not a penny came from Pili. Eventually I took him to court.

I booked passage on Iberia Airlines with five suitcases and swore I would never fly with them again. They squeezed every penny out me they could. When I left Madrid, my heart was heavy. I resented everyone, even my mother, and blamed her for some of my troubles. It was unfair but I did it anyway. At the airport the Iberia staff charged me for overweight luggage. I could barely spare the money. Then in Rome I transferred flights and no one questioned the weight of my bags. The Alitalia crew treated me with courtesy. They were better than my own countrymen had been.

Eighteen years of hard work to get a home. Gone in twelve months. I came back to Sydney with nothing. My family was waiting and that helped. One of my sons handed me a thousand dollars at the airport. Enough to buy a car. We stayed with one of my daughters while I found my footing. The warmth at home was good after the cold I had left behind. My brother-in-law Don said I should apply for housing commission. I had nothing to lose. I applied and we got a flat in Croydon Park. I found work as a boiler maker and welder. It was a new start.

Years before, after her accident, Jean had hired a solicitor. She dropped the case when we moved to Spain but back in Sydney the solicitor reopened it. Six months later the court gave her twelve thousand dollars. We were too old to buy another house, instead I suggested we go to San Francisco to see her sister, Pattie. I felt guilty about Pattie. Years ago, I had gone to see Bob in Woolloomooloo, the Mexican I met from my seafaring days. That's where I met Jean. Bob was married to Pattie, Jean's sister, then. Later I encouraged Bob to take his family to the United States. Life there had been hard for Pattie, and I thought the trip might help make things right.

One of my daughters, Linda, had chosen a boy in Spain, Juan. A hippie I thought, one among twenty million others. I had my doubts, but Juan followed her to Australia and they married. He turned out to be a good man and a loving husband. I had been wrong about him. My youngest son, René, had come with us to Spain and studied classical guitar there. Eventually he went back to Spain. That left just our youngest daughter at home.

We booked a flight to San Francisco for the three of us on Continental Airlines. The plane had mechanical trouble, so they put us on a Japanese airline instead. We landed in Tokyo and at the airport a car took us to one of the city's best hotels. Continental paid for everything. The next afternoon they put us on a plane to San Francisco. When I got there the city disappointed me.

I expected to see beautiful Hollywood dropouts, but the streets were ordinary. We stayed a month and the only beauty I saw was in the Black women. They carried themselves with elegance and style. Australian girls. I thought, would win any beauty contest with American girls. During the war in Europe I had seen American soldiers desperate for female company. I never understood it until now. The beaches in America were nothing compared to Australia's. White Americans could be sarcastic. Black Americans were courteous and went out of their way to help. After a month I wanted to go home. There is no place like home. I had learned that through many trials.

Back in Sydney I got my old job at the shipyard by the waterfront. The children were grown and gone. Life was good. Every weekend Jean and I went to the local clubs making up for lost time. For the first time in our lives, we had money saved. Not a fortune but enough to give us a bit of peace of mind. We could take care of ourselves and would not need to rely on our children. We had a car and nice clothes. The rent was high, though. I thought to myself that I could afford it now but what about later? After two years submitting my application, the Housing Commission sent me a letter. They had found us a house with a much lower rent.

When I first came to Australia the first place I went to was a brothel at 26 Forbes Street in Woolloomooloo. Now the Commission gave me a house at 28 Forbes Street. The government had taken over all the houses in that area and fixed them up. I started at 26 Forbes Street. I lived in Seven Hills for eighteen years. Now I was back. Just two doors down. I had gone to Spain. Then to Japan. Then to America. In the end I settled next door to where I started in Australia.

Number 28 Forbes Street in Woolloomooloo. It was close to everything in the city. It felt right being back.

At the shipyard, while welding a ship's plate, I fell into the water and injured my back. The pain was bad but I reported the incident and continued to work. I relied on painkillers to get through the shifts because the job was too valuable to give up. Then the union pushed for a thirty-five-hour workweek. The response was swift. The last twenty employees hired, me included, were laid off. After four years of the riskiest tasks, I found myself unemployed again.

My back ached terribly, yet I refused to burden a new employer with my injury. I went to the doctor instead. After X-rays, he confirmed my spine was bent and the discs were out of place. He sent my case for workers' payments. I got full weekly money, which was lucky, but they bound me in plastic, later a corset. No dancing, no outings, life dulled down again. Having always worked, being idle chafed at me. I had time now to watch things I had not noticed before.

Before television, Sydney thrummed with life. The streets bustled with people. But after television arrived, something changed. Post-six o'clock, the streets emptied, homes darkened. The city became like a cemetery. During my time stuck at home, I watched this happen. By day, Sydney had good shops and beautiful beaches. But at night, it became a ghost town. People were captives in their darkened living rooms, eyes fixed on flickering screens.

I remembered the weekends with my wife at the clubs before the accident. We heard good singers there with real talent. They sang for little or nothing while they waited for their big break. At home I turned on the television. American variety shows. Bad copies of what was on in the States. I recognized one of the singers from the clubs lip-syncing to an American song. The real Australian singers were still in the clubs, performing for beer money.

Nothing was truly yours here.

The commission house on Forbes Street was mine, but it wasn't. I paid every month. I would pay until I died. Then someone else would pay. No one truly owns land in Australia. You pay land tax forever. If you fail to pay the rates, the council sells your property. It's like buying a suit but having to pay continuously to wear it. The suit you never own.

I needed something I could own.

Bored and seeking sanity, I bought a second-hand typewriter and a dictionary. I started writing short stories. My grasp of English—and Spanish for that matter—wasn't perfect due to my lack of formal education, but I managed twenty-six tales. In the world of writing, you fill a room with rejections before hitting it right. Persistence is how you prove yourself. I was driven by the need to show my children, after years apart, that their father hadn't wasted his life. Maybe they thought I was a failure. I aimed to show them otherwise. It was tough writing in a second language, unable to fully express my deepest thoughts. Yet I wrote for the love of it, hoping that maybe, just maybe, someone would value my stories long after I was gone.

20

FRANCO'S LAST LAUGH

After four years on workers' compensation, the court settled my case and I received a lump sum. The money wasn't enough to buy a home, but I needed to return to Spain. René had married there while studying guitar, committed to his music and his daughter. I wanted to see my granddaughter, and the compo money would get me there. And it would keep me there long enough to see if there was interest in my stories. I had the twenty-six of them, maybe someone would read them. But René mattered more.

He had grown to love Spain, and with a daughter and steady work in music his life was there. He was committed to staying, bound by his love for his daughter and his lifelong pursuit of music.

Franco died in 1975. Now Spain wanted into Europe. They called it democracy now. But Franco's men still held office. The war criminals from the Civil War grew old in comfort, unbothered by the million they'd killed. Now these same men hunt ETA, the Basque Country and Freedom organisation, and call them terrorists. Anyone fighting for justice gets labelled—Communist, terrorist, the name doesn't matter. But I knew where ETA came from. The Republic, the legitimate government. During the war they fought as

Maquis in France, alongside the Allies. Then politics turned dirty. After the war, the world recognized Franco's regime, and the freedom fighters became terrorists.

Who are the real terrorists? I knew the answer, but no one wanted to hear it. ETA wanted justice for the dead—a million of them. They'd waited for the world to act. The world did nothing. So they acted themselves. The newspapers called them murderers. The government called them communists. But I remembered Guernica. A market day in a small town. The German planes came and bombed it flat. Women, children, livestock—everything burned. Picasso painted it so the world wouldn't forget. But the world forgot anyway. Three years of bombardments after that. Night and day. They called that justice back then. Now they call a different name.

René and I visited Toledo and travelled up to the Alcázar. The fortress sat atop the mountain, its walls thick and high. During the Civil War, Franco's troops held it from inside while the Republicans attacked uphill. A small force with bazookas could hold back a battalion from up there. The high ground meant everything. Inside the castle, they had photographs on the walls. Franco's fighters. Each one labelled a national hero. I stood there looking at them. These were the men who'd won. History tells it their way now.

Other visitors stood nearby. I said what I was thinking, that these men should answer for what they'd done. That calling them heroes was a lie.

They sighed. "If that's the case, the killings will never stop in Spain."

"But if you don't bring these people to justice," I said, "who's to prevent another civil war? The victor doesn't have to answer for anything. Look at the Jews. They still hunt war criminals. If they didn't, it would happen again. Now people think twice before raising a hand against a Jew."

They had no answer for that.

Franco haunted Spain for forty years. When death finally came for him, his ailments could have killed a horse. The doctors kept trying but he wouldn't die. It seemed Heaven wouldn't take him and Hell wouldn't have him either, so he stayed in Spain, suffering. Maybe that was the price he paid.

But he managed one last act of defiance. With prisoners for labour, he built his own tomb—a monument to himself, paid for with the suffering of others. That was no justice and no Spaniard forgets the Civil War. Spain was never communist, but now it just might go that way. Who gets blamed? Capitalism will. The people are tired of being exploited and that's what pushes them toward communism.

We left Spain to visit my son-in-law's family in Sicily. We took the train, wanting to see the landscape at a slower pace. It seemed like a good plan. It wasn't. Sure, we started well enough as we bought first-class tickets from Madrid to Palermo. It was smooth until Barcelona, where we switched trains and everything was fine until we crossed into France. At the border, a porter stole my documents. He took most of them but left the passport. As the train pulled away, I stood there and realized I was helpless and reported it to the train inspector.

Then we boarded another train. I had never seen one like it. Worse than the trains they used in the war to move prisoners. The journey to Palermo took forty-eight hours with no food. There was no dining car and the water was bad. The train stopped at every station from the French border to Palermo, crawling down Italy's coast. We saw all of Italy. But we saw it hungry.

The journey back was just as bad until we reached the Spanish border. There we saw a Japanese tourist in distress, shouting in English that a porter had stolen her handbag with two thousand dollars in it. I went to one of the plainclothes policemen and asked him to search for the porter. He told me to shut up. I knew the Spanish police so I shut up. Later, in Australia, I wrote to the Spanish authorities about how the country was run. I suspected some of the police worked with the porters, splitting what they stole from tourists.

Once we crossed into Spain, we boarded the Talgo train. It was a joy to travel on a real train again after what we'd endured. The Talgo moved swift and smooth over the rails, and we arrived in Madrid before we knew it. The contrast with the Italian nightmare was stark.

We stayed in Madrid for a while, seeing René and the granddaughter, then took the bus to Lisbon. Portugal was different from Spain, quieter, and we enjoyed the change. When we returned to Madrid, it felt good to be back. The city had gotten into our blood.

One morning we stopped at a bar for a drink, just briefly. We weren't there long. But when we came out, I reached for my wallet and found that my money was gone. A pickpocket had lifted it without me feeling a thing. Later I learned the thief was an old woman who worked that neighbourhood. She must have had hands like a surgeon. She could have made a fortune in Australia with skill like that.

Spain had taken what it wanted from me. The stories stayed in my suitcase, unread. René stayed, devoting himself to his daughter and his music. I had seen my granddaughter. I had seen Spain again, the country that made me and the country that Franco had broken. That would have to be enough.

21

HOPE IS A HABIT

Back in Australia, the days come one after another. I want to see my other children again and after that, I will be ready for whatever comes. The work is hard to find now, but Jean and I manage. The back still hurts from the old injury, but it does not stop me. I write short stories in the afternoons. They are not for money. They are not for fame. They are something for me to do with my hands and my mind. Maybe someone will read them after I am gone. Maybe they will find something there. Maybe not. Some drown their sorrows with the bottle. If that were my way, I would be drunk every day but I watched my father and saw what drink can do to a man. So I write instead and put the feelings down on paper. It keeps me steady.

When I first landed in Woolloomooloo, the neighbours were all Australians by birth. Mrs. Amble next door would bring over a meat pie if she'd made extra. You could leave your door unlocked at night. Once I locked myself out and climbed through the window at two in the morning. No one called the police. Those neighbours left long ago. The

Ambles moved out to the suburbs and the house went to a family from somewhere else. I don't know where exactly. They keep to themselves, and I keep to myself. In Madrid, before the war, the neighbours in our building looked after each other because they had to. If someone didn't come home, you went looking. If a door stayed locked too long, you knocked. That was how you survived. At sea we depended on the man working next to you. If he didn't do his job right, you might not come home. Everyone understood that. We locked nothing on the ship. There was nowhere to go and no reason to hide anything. Last week someone tried my door handle at night. I heard it turn. I got up and checked but whoever it was had gone. Now I lock the door before bed and check it twice. Sometimes I check it a third time.

A neighbourhood watch was set up to help with community safety. Twelve of us signed up. At the first meeting everyone came then at the second meeting, eight came. By the third month it was me and old Mr. Patterson down the road who could barely walk. Last month someone broke into the house on the corner. It was three in the afternoon. I was home and I heard the glass break and went to the window. Two other neighbours were at their windows. We looked but no one went outside. No one called the police until the thieves drove away. I joined to prevent crime and not just to report it. But I was wrong about that.

They tore down much of old Woolloomooloo and built new homes. The new homes are better and the people keep their yards good and their gates locked. But I see more dogs than children. The dogs are fat, and the yards are clean. Sometimes I watch the locals and think they do not appreciate it. They came with nothing and now they act like they own everything. Then I remember I came the same way. From Spain with a suitcase and the clothes I wore. My country was torn apart and Australia took me in. Someone gave me work. Someone helped me. I wanted Australia to sustain me. I expected it. Maybe that is what makes me angry. I see myself in them and I do not like it.

Jean tells me I complain too much. She is right. I complain about the noise and the traffic and the way things have changed. I complain about my back and the price of bread and the weather. She listens and then she tells me to stop.

"You're alive," she says. "That is something."

She is right about that too.

Some days are better. On Tuesdays I walk to the shops and buy the newspaper. The man at the newsstand knows my name. He came from Calabria twenty-five years ago. We talk about the weather and the European Champions Cup. He has three children, and they all went to university. I am happy for him. When I tell him that I mean it. On the walk back I see the children going to school. They are loud and they push each other and they laugh. I remember my own children at that age. How they ran everywhere, how they could not sit still. How their mother would get cross with them and I would laugh. I miss that. The children here speak different languages. I hear Greek and Italian and something I do not recognize. At first this bothered me. Now I listen and I think it is not so different from when I was young. In Madrid we had Catalans and Basques and Galicians. Everyone spoke their own way. We understood each other when we needed to.

At home I write about Spain. I write about the ships and the sea. I write about coming here and the early days when everything was hard but new and bold. The writing helps. It keeps the memories alive and clear. Some memories I want to keep and some I want to forget but they all come back when I write. I wonder if my children will read these stories. I wonder if they will understand. I left them to work, and I worked to keep them fed. Maybe they do not see it that way. Maybe they think I left because I wanted to. That is not true but maybe the truth does not matter anymore. Jean says I should not worry about it. She says they know I love them. I hope she is right. Hope is a strange thing. It does not go away even when you know better.

Going back, for years I wanted to see my other children. They were in America with their mother. I sent money when I could but it was never enough. I had seven children here to feed and clothe and send to school. The mortgage had to be paid. There was never anything left over for a ticket to America. I thought about it every day. I would lie awake at night doing the calculations. The airfare cost more than I made in three months. Even if I saved everything there were always emergencies. A child got sick. The car broke down. The roof leaked. The money disappeared.

Jean knew. She saw me lying awake. She never said anything, but she knew.

One day someone in Seven Hills told me about the British soccer pools: Littlewoods in England. You picked teams and if they drew you won money. Big money. Enough to fly to America and back. I sent for the forms. Every week Littlewoods mailed three coupons to my house. I filled them out and sent a money order back to England. Then I waited. I checked the results every Monday in the newspaper. I did this for five years. Every week I imagined winning and flying to America. I would see my children. I would take them to dinner and we would talk and they would understand why I had to leave. They would forgive me.

One Monday I arrived at work early to check the results. I had eight crosses. Twenty-four points. My legs shook and I could not stand still. I asked another worker to check the numbers. He checked and there were twenty-four points.

I had won.

I went home and sent a telegram to England. It cost three pounds, six dollars. That was a lot of money then but I didn't care. The neighbours heard the news and we had a party. The party cost a small fortune but I did not care about that either. Then the envelope came from England. I could not open it. My hands shook too much. I gave it to Jean. She said no because I had won it and I should open it.

I opened it.

The check was for thirty-five shillings. Forty million people in England had won. We all had twenty-four points and we all split the pool. I was sick for a week. I could not eat. I could not sleep. Jean tried to comfort me but there was nothing to say. After a week I bought more coupons and kept playing. What else could I do? I had come this far and I could not stop now.

Some people would say this is foolish. Playing the same numbers week after week. Year after year. Spending money we do not have on a dream that will never come. Maybe they are right. But I think of the old story about the man who tried to swim across a river. Halfway across he got tired. He turned back and drowned. I am more than halfway across now and cannot turn back. The only way to win is to keep going. That is all I know how to do.

Hope is a habit. You cannot break it even when you want to.

22

NOWHERE LEFT TO GO

I had saved some money for rainy days. Not much but enough. At sixty-three I could not wait anymore. I had not seen my other children in forty years. The pools had not worked. Nothing else would work either and it was time to go. I wrote them a letter saying I wanted to visit. I told them I had saved money for the ticket but I did not say it had taken me forty years to save it. Then I waited for their reply.

I should have gone sooner. The money was always tight but that was not the real reason. The real reason was fear. What if I knocked on the door and they did not know me? What if they said we don't know you? What if they closed the door? That would cut deep, deeper than anything else could cut. I thought about this every day while I waited for the letter. Jean said they would be happy to see me, that they were my children and would remember. But I was not sure. Forty years is a long time. They were small when I left and now they had their own lives. Maybe they did not need a father anymore.

Nobody is perfect and we all make mistakes. But some of us pay a higher price than others and I count myself among those who paid. But I had made my choice. I wrote the letter. I could not take it back now. All I could do was wait.

In the United States I have two sons and a daughter who have given me eighteen grandchildren and three great-grandchildren. I have never met most of them. My first wife remarried an American after the divorce and moved the family from England to the United States. They grew up there and made lives I know only from letters. One of my sons joined the army went to Vietnam and used the money to study medicine. Now he is a dermatologist, a good one from what I hear. My other son manages a large factory and has done well for himself. They both succeeded in ways I never could.

My daughter is different. When she visited us in Spain years ago I expected to see the little girl I remembered, but a thirty-six-year-old woman stood at the door and looked at me like I was a stranger. Maybe I was. We did not talk much during that visit and she carried something heavy inside her that I could see but did not know how to address. What do you say to a daughter you have not seen in thirty years? She left after three days and we have not spoken since.

I worked twelve hours a day in Australia, sometimes more, thinking hard work would make everything right. I believed if I worked hard enough I could save enough money to bring them all together, but hard work and basic wages do not make you rich. They keep you alive and that is all. I learned this too late.

One night in April I was writing at the kitchen table while everyone slept. The house was quiet and then I felt something in the room. Not a sound or a movement but a presence. I stopped writing and sat very still. A voice said wake up before it is too late. I do not know if the voice was in the room or in my head or if I imagined it, but I knew what it meant. Time was running out. That is when I decided to write the letter.

The next day I went to the bank and withdrew our savings. Then I went to the travel agency and booked two tickets to New Orleans with a stop in San Francisco on Continental Airlines. The same airline had once flown us to Japan by mistake when we tried to go somewhere else. This time we would go to New Orleans. The flight was set for June 7.

I sent a letter to my son telling him we were coming. I did not know if he believed me. After all these years why would he? My father used to say the world was not made out of cowards. I thought about that while I waited for his reply. The words gave me courage to keep going and we started buying gifts for everyone and packing our bags. We had six weeks until the flight and the days passed slowly. Jean was nervous about the trip and I could see the worry in her face when she thought I was not looking. She did not know how our sons would receive her after so many years. I told her it would be fine but I was not sure myself.

Then a letter came from my son. They would be waiting for us at the airport. It had been forty years since I last saw them. Forty years. My granddaughter had invited us to her wedding in Indiana and we bought her a present. Jean held the letter and cried, and I thought everything would work out after all. But the night before the flight Jean fell very ill. She could not get out of bed and her skin was hot to the touch. I called a taxi and we went to the hospital. The doctor examined her and his face was serious when he came out. She needed to be hospitalized immediately. She could not travel and she could not get on the plane.

I stood in the hospital corridor and did not know what to do. Everything had been arranged. My son was expecting us and my granddaughter was getting married. After forty years

I was finally going and now I could not go. Jean looked at me from the hospital bed and said go without me. I said no. She said I had waited too long and I should go. I said I would not leave her. We argued about it but I would not change my mind. So, I stayed.

The doctors said Jean should stay in the hospital for at least a week, maybe longer. They said I should cancel her ticket and fly alone and she could follow when she was better. This was not what I wanted. After forty years of waiting I did not want to see my sons alone, but there was no other choice. So I went alone. I boarded the plane to New Orleans on Saturday morning with my one suitcase and the gifts we had bought. The seat next to me was empty where Jean should have been sitting. I looked at it and thought about turning back, but the plane was already moving.

On the plane they gave me forms to fill out. How long would I stay in the United States? I wrote "It all depends" because I did not know. Maybe a week. Maybe longer. It depended on many things. My itinerary included a stop in San Francisco to visit my sister-in-law. She was married to the Mexican I had first met in Sydney years ago. They had four sons and two were born in Australia and two in America. I had helped raise the eldest when he was small. I had been close to him once.

When I arrived in San Francisco they picked me up at the airport. My sister-in-law was warm and welcoming but her eldest son, the one I had helped raise, barely looked at me. He shook my hand but there was nothing behind it. No recognition. No warmth. He treated me like a stranger his mother had brought home. I stayed three days and he did not speak to me once unless his mother made him. At dinner he ate quickly and left the table. When I tried to talk to him about the old days, he said he did not remember. Maybe he did not. Maybe he just did not want to. I could not sleep that night at my sister-in-law's house. The bed was comfortable but I lay awake thinking about the nephew who would not look at me and about my sons waiting in New Orleans.

At five in the morning on the third day I got up and dressed and packed my bag. My sister-in-law was already awake. She did not allow smoking in the house so we stood in the yard while I smoked a cigarette and she apologized again for her son. I told her not to worry. People change and forty years is a long time. I understood that now. I thanked her, took a taxi to the airport and arrived by quarter to six. The flight to New Orleans left at eight. I sat in the departure area and drank coffee and smoked and tried not to think about what would happen when I landed. Forty years is a long time, maybe too long.

On the plane I could not sit still. My hands shook when I tried to read the newspaper. I kept thinking about what I would say when I saw them. Would they recognize me? Would I recognize them? What if they looked at me the way the nephew had looked at me, with nothing in their eyes? When the plane landed I walked slowly through the terminal. I did not want to rush and wanted to prepare myself for whatever would happen next. Then I came through the gate and saw them standing there together, watching the passengers come out.

They were there. Both of them waiting for me.

I walked toward them and one of them saw me first. He said something to his brother and they both started walking. Then we were together and they were shaking my hand and pulling me close and talking at once. Their voices were deep and their hands were strong and they were glad to see me. I could tell they were glad. After forty years they were still my sons and they still wanted to see me and that was all that mattered.

I had booked a hotel in New Orleans before leaving Sydney. This turned out to be wise because Ricardo, my doctor son, was going through a divorce and his house was too small for visitors. He owned a good house but the divorce was messy and he lived now in a modest flat. American divorce laws are hard on men and he had lost almost everything. The divorce had kept him quiet all these years. Maybe he thought I had abandoned him and maybe the divorce made him understand what it means to lose your family. Now he was warm to me and we talked like we had not talked before. Old wounds were healing but slowly.

Ricardo took a week off work to spend with me. My other son Rafael came down from Pennsylvania where he managed a factory. We spent the days together walking around New Orleans and eating in restaurants and talking about everything except the past. We did not need to talk about the past. Being together was enough. My daughter Gloria was in Russia and did not come. She had visited me in Spain years ago and she was cold then and nothing had changed. Some wounds do not heal. I understood that.

After five days I started to miss Jean. I called her at the hospital every night but it was not the same as having her there. Then on the sixth day Ricardo drove me to the airport and she came through the gate. She was pale and thin but she was smiling. The doctors had let her travel. She met my sons and they were good to her and she cried when she hugged them. We all cried a little then we went back to Ricardo's flat and Jean cooked dinner the way she always did and we sat around the table like a family. It was not perfect, but it was good. It was enough.

We had nowhere left to go but forward.

On Monday Ricardo went back to his medical practice and Rafael drove north to Pennsylvania. We stayed in New Orleans a few more days but Ricardo had patients to see, and hospital rounds to make. He worked long hours and came home tired. We ate dinner together but after dinner he had to study medical journals and return phone calls. His life was full and busy and there was little room in it for visitors. I could see this and Jean could see it too. We had come to see my sons and now we had seen them. It was time to go. We decided to visit Rafael in Pennsylvania before returning to Australia.

We bought two train tickets on the Crescent. I wanted to see where Rafael lived and meet his family. The ticket agent told us the journey would take more than thirty hours, but I did not understand how far it was. I thought Pennsylvania was close to New Orleans. I was clearly wrong. The train left New Orleans in the morning, and we rode all day and all night and into the next day. We went through Mississippi and saw Hattiesburg and Meridian pass by the window. Then Alabama and Birmingham where we stopped for a while. Then Atlanta where the train sat at the station and more passengers got on. After Atlanta we went through the Carolinas. Greenville and Charlotte and Greensboro. The names went by and the landscape changed. Jean and I sat by the window and watched.

In Louisiana everything was flat and green. In Alabama there were more hills. By the time we reached the mountains of North Carolina and Virginia the train was climbing higher and the air through the window was cooler. We passed through Lynchburg and Charlottesville in Virginia. Then the train went to Washington and Baltimore and finally Philadelphia where we changed for Pittsburgh.

I had not realised the United States was so big. On the map it looked small but on the train it went on forever. We rode for more than thirty hours and passed through seven states, and we were still in the same country. It made Australia seem small by comparison. We reached Pittsburgh Station at one in the morning, after two days on the train. There, waiting for us, were my granddaughter—who had kept in touch through letters—and my daughter-in-law. It was a happy reunion. From there, we drove four hours to Rafael's farm, a remote place surrounded by bush and trees, isolated in the heart of the countryside.

The next day Dorothy, my first wife and the mother of my sons and daughter, came to the farm. She was polite to Jean and she shook her hand and smiled and asked about the journey from Australia. But I could see something stony behind her smile. She looked at Jean the way you look at someone who has taken something that belonged to you. Jean saw it too but she said nothing.

Dorothy came to visit every evening after that and she never said why she came. She would sit with us for an hour or two and talk about small things like the weather and the farm and the grandchildren. Then she would leave. The grandchildren were polite to her but distant. They did not know her well and they did not seem interested in knowing her better. She sat alone at one end of the table and they sat at the other end. Her husband had died two years before and I could see the loneliness in her.

Rafael and his wife worked long hours. They left early in the morning and came home late. Most evenings it was just Jean and me and Dorothy sitting in the farmhouse with nothing to say to each other. We had travelled all the way from Australia to be with my sons but my sons were working and we were alone. The farm was very isolated and dense woods surrounded it on all sides. The nearest town was twenty miles away. You needed a car to go anywhere. Even to buy groceries you had to drive twenty miles. Without a car you were trapped there. After a week all the towns in Pennsylvania looked the same to me. One main street and one store and one gas station. Trees everywhere. The same houses and the same fields. It went on like that for miles in every direction.

I had travelled to see my sons and I hoped we would talk about the past and clear things up. But no one mentioned it. The divorce and the years apart and all the things that had happened stayed unspoken. I thought about bringing it up but I decided not to. Sometimes it is better to leave things alone.

Dorothy seemed tense and uncomfortable when she came to visit. I could see it in the way she held herself and the way she did not look at me directly. But she never said anything. Maybe she was afraid they would turn her away if she made trouble. So she sat quietly and spoke only when spoken to.

When she arrived they were polite. My sons and their wives nodded and said hello. The grandchildren were polite too but they kept their distance. No one asked her many questions. No one sat with her for long. After a few minutes someone would excuse themselves. Then another would leave. Soon it was just Jean and me sitting with her at the table and we talked about small things until it was time for her to go. She drove from house to house in her old car and no one invited her to stay. She was always leaving. I watched this and it hurt me to see. She was their mother and their grandmother. Whatever she had done in the past she was still that.

Jean was my wife now and I loved her but Dorothy was the mother of my sons and I could not forget that. The way the whole family kept their distance from her made me sad. But I said nothing about it, it was not my place anymore. I had made my choices and they had made theirs. But it saddened me to see how little warmth there was in that house.

One of the great-grandchildren ran to Jean and put her arms around her and called her grandmother. She did this right in front of Dorothy. It was a hard moment. I watched

Dorothy watch this and I wondered what she felt. I would not have liked it if I were her. But I had no ill will toward her. She had kept our children out of foster care after I was deported from England. That took strength and I respected her for it. We had both made mistakes. The mistakes were long past, and the hate had turned to regret. I wanted to tell her to sell what she had and go back to England. Some in her family might welcome her there. Better that than staying here alone with no one who seemed to want her around. But I could not say this. If I said it she might think I still cared about her in some way. So I said nothing.

I have found happiness with Jean and the family around me. Dorothy moves from house to house and no one wants her to stay. It is hard to watch. You see a life coming apart slowly and there is nothing you can do. In America some say that they send old people to nursing homes. I heard this from several people and I saw it was true. You spend your whole life raising children and then when you are old they put you in a home with strangers. This is what they call taking care of their parents. It made me want to go back to Australia. This could happen to me, it could happen to anyone. I thought about Dorothy and I thought this is how I might end up if I were to stay in America.

I once knew three sisters in Australia. They were good-looking women and they never married. They stayed home and took care of their parents until the parents died. I do not want that for my children. I do not want them to give up their lives for me. But they would not put me in a home with strangers either. That is the difference. In Australia people still take care of their own. In America everyone is too busy.

After ten days at the farm, I felt restless. The isolation was getting to me. The days were all the same. We woke up. We ate breakfast. Rafael and his wife went to work. Jean and I sat in the house or drove to the shops or walked in the bush.

Then they came home late and we ate dinner and went to bed. The same thing every day. One night Rafael came home at midnight. I was still awake. I wanted to talk to him about things. I had travelled all this way to see him and we had barely spoken. But when he came in he turned on the television and sat watching it. I tried to talk to him and he answered but his eyes stayed on the screen. After a while I gave up and went to bed. The grandchildren were the same way, polite but not interested. They had their own lives and I was just an old man visiting from Australia. I could feel that I was in the way there. The wedding was still twelve days away. Twelve more days of sitting in that farmhouse with nothing to do and no one to talk to. Jean never complained but I could see she was tired of it too. The same drives to the same shops. The same walks in the same bush. This was not what I came to America for.

America was not like the movies. The places we visited all looked the same to me. Small towns. A few shops. Not much else. I had expected more. We drove through forests for miles. Trees on both sides of the road as far as you could see. America has vast forests and timber wealth but they do not seem to use it. Instead, Americans travel to other countries and tell them how to develop their natural resources. I found this strange.

We drove through a place called Oil City. They discovered oil there many years ago and you could smell it when the wind blew a certain way. The smell came up from underground. Rafael said it would cost too much to extract it now but the oil was still there. If they extracted it there would be jobs and money but they left it in the ground.

With the wedding more than a week away, I needed to get away from the farm. I thought about going to Tijuana for a few days and then coming back to Indiana for the wedding. My son did not like this idea. He could not understand why

I would not want to spend another twelve days waiting on the farm. He suggested I go to Virginia first and visit another daughter and the one getting married. He said I could travel with her to Indiana from Virginia and then on to Tijuana if I still wanted.

I wanted to see Tijuana because I had translated some of my stories into Spanish. I thought it would be good to try my luck there. In the end, we agreed that I would go to Virginia first. It was ten hours from Pennsylvania. I did not care. At that point I would have agreed to go anywhere just to leave the farm behind. So we drove to Virginia.

The drive from Pittsburgh to Virginia took ten hours. There was nothing to see but forests along the road. We arrived in Virginia late in the day. I met more of my grandchildren, but there was no warmth and I was disappointed. My reason for coming to America was to see my two sons. After that, I saw no reason to stay longer. We spent one day in Virginia. The next day we set out for Indiana, twelve hours on the road with my granddaughter, the one getting married. She rode with us. She did not say much, and the miles went slow. Her fiancé met us in Indiana. He was no warmer than she was. I asked him to take us to Indianapolis so we would be close to the airport. He agreed but did not like it. He dropped us at a run-down hotel on the edge of the city and drove away barely saying goodbye. We checked in, glad at least to be finished with the journey.

I decided not to wait for the wedding. There was no point staying eight more days in that hotel. Pain started in my shoulders the next morning. I thought about going to Tijuana but the cost of seeing a doctor here was too high. I changed our tickets and we flew back to Australia. When I landed I found needed surgery on my neck—ten stitches. I had been smoking almost two packs a day for fifty-two years. The doctor told me to quit and I did. I have not touched a cigarette since.

These days in Indianapolis showed me the real state of things. My granddaughter never came to visit and the distance with the family was plain. Maybe it was what I needed to see. On the way home I thought about how lives fall apart in small ways. Sometimes there is no fixing things, only moving on.

23

CARRYING ON

Back in Australia, I kept my head down. Quiet years teach their own courage, and then the phone rings. Four years after returning from the States, a call from my sister in Madrid brought grim news: my mother was dying. My family told me to see her while I still could. With what I'd saved, I bought a ticket to Madrid and reached her bedside two days later, surrounded by doctors, nurses, and a priest with the last rites. The past does not close like a door. It leaves a draft.

My visit to Spain caught everyone off guard. When someone at the hospital told my mother who I was, her eyes fluttered open despite the pain. I could not bear to watch her suffer and said so to her doctor. He pulled a syringe from his drawer, handed it to me, and said, "Here, do it yourself."

At night, I sat by her side. During the day, I saw my son's daughter, who told me she didn't like me. I said I didn't like her either, though I didn't mean it. It stung. Over time, my mother's spirits lifted. She even had the staff laughing with her poetry. Some credited me with her recovery, but after a month, I had to leave. That was the last time I saw her.

When words fail, we measure love in minutes. A year after I returned to Spain to see my mother for the last time, she passed away. Despite her pain, she died content, knowing I had come so far to be with her. Before I left, my youngest sister, living comfortably yet alone, handed me an expensive watch, a memento of my journey.

In the end, family stays complicated. But I have no sermon , only what time has taught me. We love, we hurt, we forgive, we carry on. I wonder what stories my grandchildren will tell of the life I had. Looking back, I wonder if it's destiny or choice. Did I choose this winding road, or was it chosen for me? Did I learn the lessons, or am I still searching? I cannot answer. Perhaps in the end, it's enough to have lived, to have struggled, to have loved as I could.

What remains is small in the hand, large in the heart. Each night I wind my sister's watch. Its ticking is steady; mine is not. Dust and stars, work and hunger, love and hurt—I carried them as I could. The rest belongs to those who remember. There are things a man can only say once he is almost done. Whatever I failed to say, I leave to my children to answer.

Alfonso Mora Almenara
Maroubra
1993

A Letter to My Father

Dear Dad,

I've been trying to work out how to write this. Not as a boy to a father, not as a man trying to make sense of what he inherited but just as someone who still carries you around, in memory and in blood and in all the conversations we never finished.

There was always music between us. The songs you played - Cuban son, Argentinian tango, Spanish flamenco, canciones Española, paso doble - were the soundtrack I grew up inside. When I hear them now, I'm back in those rooms, and I know without having to think about it that I was loved. I never doubted that. What I understand, that I didn't then, is what those songs meant to you - the elegance in them, the ache, that particular defiant joy. You were homesick for something you couldn't name, and the music was the closest you could get.

I knew you as a storyteller before I knew you as anything else. The stories of Spain, the civil war, the wandering - they shaped how I understood the world long before I understood them. Only when I read your memoirs properly did I see the full picture: how much more there was beneath what you told us, like the currents beneath that stolen rowboat as you tried to row the English Channel alone in the dark. You told us the story. You didn't always tell us what it cost.

Our closeness had its seasons. I felt nearest to you when I was small, when your world was still the whole world. As I got older something shifted - partly the natural distance between a father and a grown son finding his own way, partly something harder to name. You were shaped by a time and a place that made you who you were: your sense of honour, the way you understood what a man was supposed to be. I came of age in the sixties with different ideas about most of that. We loved each other across that gap, but we didn't always know how to say so.

I wish I had spoken more clearly in those last weeks. When you showed me the letter from De Gaulle, a personal letter, thanking you for your service with the Free French, I didn't say what I should have said. That it mattered. That I was proud of you. That the boy who forged his father's signature to get onto a truck full of volunteers, who ended up fighting in Syria at sixteen, who stood in a lineup and was commended by de Gaulle himself - that boy was extraordinary, and I should have told you I knew it. When you spoke about the things you regretted, the people you'd hurt, I should have told you that regret like that is its own kind of reckoning, and that I understood more than you knew.

And I should have asked you about my name. Manolete. I carried it as both a pride and a puzzle for most of my life. A schoolyard in Sydney's western suburbs is a long way from the bullrings of Spain, Dad. I know what you meant by it, your tribute, your challenge, your way of handing something fierce and proud across the distance between your world and mine. I understand that now. Thank you for it, even for the bewildering years.

What I claimed from you, consciously or not: the restlessness, the love of music, the political instincts, the refusal to be quiet when something was wrong. What I kept my distance from: the stubbornness, the temper, the closed doors. I was sometimes afraid of you. Mostly I was warmed by you. That's probably about right for a father and son.

You pursued women your whole life, not always wisely, not always kindly. I won't pretend otherwise. But I don't think it was only appetite. I think you were looking for something, some version of home or recognition or ease that kept eluding you. Sometimes you found it briefly. Often you left hurt behind. I'm not judging. I'm just saying I see it more clearly now than I did.

You raised seven children on a boilermaker's wage. You encouraged us to reach beyond where we'd started. You gave us music and stories and a stubbornness about living fully and you gave us that through your failures as much as your strengths. That's not nothing, Dad: that's quite a lot.

There are things I wish I'd said while I still could. This will have to do instead.

With love,

Your son,

Manolete

April
2026

EPILOGUE: WHAT ENDURES

Every one of us - Paul, Cristina, Teresa, Linda, Michelle, René, Rafael, Gloria, Ricardo, and I - has known our father in different ways. The man who emerges in these pages - adventurer, storyteller, survivor - is both familiar and, at times, elusive. His memoirs, written for all of us, were perhaps his way of explaining himself, a quiet offering of reckoning, maybe even a gesture of apology for the ways he fell short.

In the end, what mattered most was not the sum of his adventures nor the contradictions of his character, but the simple, human need to be held by love. In his final moments, lying in a hospital bed, our father called out for his mother. In his mind, she came to him. He was not alone. Our mother sat beside him. Us children were there, even those he once feared he had lost.

Rafael's plane had just touched down at Sydney Airport. Ricardo stood at his side. René had flown in from Spain. Manolete had returned to Hong Kong after seeing him. The rest of our siblings, gathered in Sydney, held vigil. He called out for Paul, his eldest, who entered our father's life not by blood but by love.

In that moment, whatever distances had lingered dissolved. His story, a life of struggle, imperfection, and longing, closed not with silence, but with presence. Together, we bore witness to his leaving. Together, we affirmed that his life mattered.

There is no neat conclusion to a life, no final line that can hold all its messiness or meaning. But we, his children, stood as testament that even the most crooked of journeys can circle home.

Paul, Manolete, Cristina, Teresa, Linda, René, and Michelle
April 2026

Acknowledgements

My father wrote this memoir for his family. Getting it into the shape it deserved became, in the end, a family effort.

My brothers and sisters - Paul, Cristina, Teresa, Linda, René and Michelle - gave me memories, photographs and pieces of history I didn't have on my own. None of us holds the whole story. We each remembered different things, kept different fragments, saw Dad differently depending on when and where our lives touched his. The book is richer for that, and I'm grateful to all of them.

I want to say something about our mother, who barely appears in these pages but made them possible in ways that go unrecorded. She gave Dad the time and space to write, and she was the steady thing behind a life that was rarely steady. That kind of presence doesn't make it onto the page, but anyone who knew them both will understand what I mean.

Thanks are also due to those who helped with the unglamorous work like scanning photographs, sorting through papers, making sense of typewritten pages that weren't always easy to read. It took the time and patience that mattered.

Finishing this book mattered to me because it mattered to my father. He had lived a remarkable and difficult life, and he wanted it written down. We felt strongly that it should be. Working through his manuscript, trying to honour his voice, his humour, his contradictions, and his hard-won understanding of himself, was something I was glad to do for him, even if I wished many times he were still here to argue with me about it.

This book is for him, and for everyone who comes from him. I hope it keeps something of his voice alive.

Manolete Mora
Sydney
April 2026

www.ingramcontent.com/pod-product-compliance
Lightning Source LLC
Chambersburg PA
CBHW031958050726
47590CB00006B/1962